Endorsements

I don't think David Harwood knows how to write a book that is not full of solid biblical reflection, deep content and wise evaluations. His perspective and advice should be received with gratitude. His writings have great credibility. This book is no exception; passionate, truthful, pastoral, and important.

Daniel Juster
Founder of Tikkun International
Israel

I'm stunned by David's research and the anti-Semitism that has infected the Church of Jesus Christ in recent centuries. I'm so grateful that voices like his are helping us recover a biblical affection for the nation of Israel. May holy love for Jesus' ethnic people fill our hearts and empower fiery intercession until Israel is the blessing to the nations she's called to be.

Bob Sorge
Author, bobsorge.com

I don't know another man who carries a greater revelation of the love of God than David Harwood. Those who hold this important book in their hand will have the opportunity to combine that revelation along with the revelation of God's love for the Jewish people. When we embrace and carry God's heart for Israel, it will give us a greater purpose and passion to express God's love to the Nations.

Scott Volk
Together for Israel
Charlotte, NC

David Harwood knows the love of God. The Father's heart for Israel and for believers today shines through each page. This book will enlighten you and stir your thinking regarding long entrenched viewpoints that dilute God's plan for Israel. Every believer should love Israel passionately, for God does. And every believer would do well to read this book! Be sure to get one more copy for a friend or a pastor. This book is so important for today!

Brian Simmons
The Passion Translation Project

As a priest in Christ's one holy "catholic" and apostolic Church for three decades, I can say with authority that the "historic" Church has been woefully ignorant of the place of "historic" Israel in God's Holy Temple. David's superb exegesis of Romans 9-11 will open one's eyes to Paul's (the Holy Spirit's) understanding of historic Israel's place in a truly unified body of Christ. As one of those "wild shoots" grafted in to "the Righteous Branch", I believe it behooves us to take a good hard look at what it will take for the whole, universal Church to be part of the answer to Jesus' prayer in John 17 that we would be one! A must read for those with a heart for authentic unity.

Father Michael Paciello, M.Div.
Charismatic Episcopal Church
Pillars of Reconciliation/Int'l Prison Chaplains Association

When God desires to restore Biblical truth to His people, He raises up voices who proclaim what is clearly written in His Word. David Harwood is one of those voices. Once we grasp these biblical truths, we own them forever, wondering why it took so long to see what is so clearly written. This happened to me many times as I read this excellent book on God's love for the Jewish people.

Charles Simpson
Oasis Christian Center
Long Island City, NY

With characteristic scholarship and thoughtfulness, David Harwood has directly addressed one of the most common and important questions asked today: what is the importance of national Israel for the New Testament Church? This book answers this question with insight, passion and sensitivity, and is a must-read for both Jewish and Gentile believers looking to understand why God loves the Jewish people today.

David Herling
English Congregation Pastor
House of the Lord Christian Church
Flushing, NY

For the Sake of the Fathers is brilliantly creative and convincingly researched. Harwood compellingly challenges 19 centuries of misconception regarding the Jewish people and Christianity. I heartily endorse this book as a healthy tonic, restoring the vibrant, God-intended, Jewish-rooted body of Messiah.

Eitan Shishkoff
Tents of Mercy
Israel

For the Sake of the Fathers

A New Testament View of God's Love for the Jewish People

David Harwood

ISBN: 978-1983406652

Published by Createspace.

Foreword

Pastor David Harwood has written a wonderful book, an encouraging book, a challenging book, a disturbing book. It is all those things because it is a truthful book, based on the eternal truths of the Word of God. By opening your heart to those truths, your own life will be enriched and changed. Are you ready for a fresh encounter with the Lord, a Word-based encounter that will open up eternal perspectives for you? Are you ready for your eyes to be opened?

David and I have been friends since the 1980s, and if there's one thing I know about David it is that he pursues the heart of God. He doesn't just want information. He wants to draw near to the Lord, to understand what is important to Him, and then to order his life accordingly. The many worship songs he has written have drawn from that same source—the heart of God—and the many teachings he has delivered, finally in book form in recent years, have also come from that source: the heart of God as revealed through His Word.

Here, in this very important book, David takes you through the New Testament writings, explaining how deeply God's heart beats for the people of Israel, examining the role of Jew and Gentile in the Church, and helping the Gentile Christian understand how deeply God loves him or her (as a Gentile, not as someone who has to become a Jew), while explaining at the same time why it is so important for Gentiles to give themselves to Israel's redemption. And, he asks, "Where is wisdom?" His answer: "I believe that wisdom discerns this: principalities of Christian anti-Semitism are at work today." If ever, then, there was a time for a book like this to be written, it is today. Will you be on God's side in this urgent hour, or on the side of those who want to destroy the Jewish people from the earth?

Once you have read this book, you will know why the battle is so pitched and why the Jewish people still matter to the Lord. As David explains so well in the pages that follow, this "is Paul's prophetic perspective: If the Jewish people's failure to receive the Messiah Jesus produces worldwide blessings, then their certain future reconciliation to their King will cause unspeakable, unimaginable blessings to burst forth. Apart from these convictions, there is no Pauline understanding of the end-times and the age-to-come. It was important to Paul. He pled with the Gentile disciples to embrace this." Precisely so.

But David does not merely write as a teacher of Scripture. He writes with the heart of a pastor, having served a congregation on Long Island for several decades. He wants to be sure that every reader, especially every Gentile reader, is grounded in God's love for them: "There is no reason," he writes, "for any Gentile to seek significance through adapting a pseudo-Jewish identity. The measure of how God values every person is Calvary (Romans 5:8)."

Yet David is not afraid to challenge us, recounting some of the ugliest facts of Church history, where Jew-hatred was often deemed compatible with following Jesus. How could this be? David also gives us a sober glimpse into the future, asking how God will judge the nations that mistreat Israel. How often do we think about this?

But above all, this is a book of life-giving truth, and David is a master of weaving together Old Testament revelation in the full light of the New Covenant Scriptures. Nowhere does he do this better than in his treatment of Romans 9-

11, in my mind, the best popular treatment I've seen of these chapters to date. (His rewriting of certain verses through the lens of replacement theology is classic.) As you take hold of these verses, you will understand Paul's anguish, which reflects God's anguish, and you will learn about the heights and depths of God's love. The Lord is ready to share that anguish and that love with each of you!

I can honestly say that, to this very moment, the Father longs to see His Jewish people recognize Yeshua (Jesus), their Messiah with a deep and intense desire. And you, as someone who knows Yeshua personally, are called to play a role in helping these lost sheep find their Shepherd, just as it was Gentile Christians who helped lead me to Him in 1971.

So, be assured that you are needed, and be assured that we need each other. Only together will we see the fullness of the purposes of God, as the greatest harvest in world history, from the nations and from the Jewish people, brings about the end of the age. Even so, come, Lord Jesus!

Dr. Michael L. Brown
Author, *Our Hands Are Stained with Blood: The Tragic Story of the 'Church' and the Jewish People*
Host, the Line of Fire radio show

Introduction

THIS BOOK'S TARGET AUDIENCE AND PURPOSE IS narrow. I'm writing to the disciple of Jesus who knows God's love and, by the power of the Holy Spirit, loves the Jewish people. Its intent is to expose that believer to some ways the New Testament speaks of God's love for Israel.

In 2008 I finished *God's True Love*, a book about God's love for every human being. In that book, I applied Biblical texts about the Creator's love for all humanity and every individual that were originally written specifically to the Jewish people. This was a legitimate application of Scripture. Why? Because part of God's purpose in choosing the Jewish people was that they might be a prophetic, priestly representation of humanity's relationship to God.

At the same time, I believe God's love for Israel is more than a metaphor. Knowing this conviction, a few friends challenged me to write about His specific love for the Jewish people.

Since I am a Jewish believer in the Messiah Jesus, I avoid specializing on this subject. I prefer it when non-Jewish believers proclaim it. Personally, I don't like being exposed to the accusation, or the temptation, of having an ethnic ax to grind. However, since I used Israel as a picture of God's love for humanity, and as a response to my friends' challenge, I felt that I owed it to the God of truth, to my people and the Church to offer my perspective and contribute to the discussion of this topic: God's Love for the Jewish People. Taking up that challenge has proven to be a perilous pilgrimage.

Revealed truth tries the heart. The realities of which I've written are no exception. Additionally, it is possible to express, or overemphasize, a truth in a way that is unhealthy, imbalanced and offensive. I hope these chapters are healthy, balanced and edifying. However, I know what I've written might provide a provocation, wound pride, and stimulate offense. It may be that the problem is not in what is written but in the affronted believer's need to be deeply rooted and grounded in God's love.

Recognizing the danger of giving offense, I've sought to be gentle as well as truthful. I've had the book vetted for truth and attitude by some Gentile Christian and Messianic Jewish leaders. I trust that in these pages God's love for each person and every ethnic group is revealed, guarded and valued. At the same time, it is up to each person to maturely deal, in the sight of God, with their reactions to what the apostles taught about God's love for the Jewish people.

If anyone wants to know what I believe concerning God's love for each person I encourage them to read *God's True Love*. That book is about God's love for everyone. That is not the topic of this book. This book is about what the apostles taught concerning God's specific love for the Jewish people.

As I deliberately studied the New Testament Scriptures on this topic I discovered: a) There is a lot more information about this than I knew. b) The Apostolic Writings (the New Testament) reveal that God's love for the Jewish people is intrinsic to the apostles' worldview. c) The revelation of God's love for Israel, viewed through the lens of the New Testament, is more intense than I imagined.

This book is not comprehensive. There is a lot more written in the Bible than is discussed in this book. Yet, it seems to me that many who love the Jewish people take their theological stand in specific verses from the Hebrew Scriptures (the Old Testament). They are not necessarily familiar with how this truth is expressed in the Apostolic Writings. I hope this book helps remedy that and reveals aspects of the unity of the Scriptures that pertain to this vital theme.

Finally, I want to add one more thing. A lie, prevalent amongst the Jewish community, is that the much-touted love many evangelicals claim to have for the Jewish people is, in fact, a scam. The lie they believe is that it may appear to be love, but that love is based solely upon self-interested delusions about the end-times. Another lie is that any love evangelicals seek to demonstrate is not real love, but an evangelistic ploy to soften up and convert Jews to Christianity. This book gives completely different, New Testament based, reasons for Christians to love the Jewish people. The call to love the Jewish people is rooted in God's heart. As you read this book you will discover more of the apostolic revelation concerning the love God has, right now, for His people.

To those who are already familiar with many of these themes, I encourage you to read this book. There may be some things here that will further inform or powerfully confirm your understandings.

> For we know in part ... (1 Corinthians 13:9a)

Contents

1

You Belong!

IN THE NEW TESTAMENT, THE JEWISH BELIEVERS IN Jesus are considered the righteous remnant of Israel. Let's look into the relationship between the Jewish Remnant and Gentiles who are called into the Messiah's Body. First, let us rehearse some ultimate realities of salvation.

To begin, everyone has an ultimate destiny and a fundamental personal identity. All believers are children of God and will be revealed as such.

> But as many as received Him, to them He gave the right to become children of God, even to those who believe in His name, who were born, not of blood nor of the will of the flesh nor of the will of man, but of God (John 1:12-13).

> Beloved, now we are children of God, and it has not appeared as yet what we will be. We know that when He appears, we will be like Him, because we will see Him just as He is (1 John 3:2).

All who know the Lord are on the same plane and have the same function. In regards to a redeemed one's status with God, there is no difference between Jews and Gentiles, bound and free, males and females, poor and rich, etc. All relate to the same Father through the same Savior and the same Spirit lives in them.

In regards to a redeemed one's status with God, there is no difference between Jews and Gentiles, bound and free, males and females, poor and rich.

> There is neither Jew nor Greek, there is neither slave nor free man, there is neither male nor female; for you are all one in Christ Jesus (Galatians 3:28).

> There is one body and one Spirit, just as also you were called in one hope of your calling; one Lord, one faith, one baptism, one God and Father of all who is over all and through all and in all (Ephesians 4:4-6).

Redeemed Jews and Gentiles comprise one Body. They are equally beloved, unified, children of God, members of the Bride and participants in the New Covenant Priesthood.

Each is called to be emotionally and socially secure within these contexts and is to supremely value his fellowship with God. It is wonderful to live without insecurity and vain competition. We are not to feel valued or devalued according to pre-resurrection identities and roles. The values of the Kingdom are right-side up, but the world's values are upside-down. Let's live coherently with reality.

> But Jesus called them to Himself and said, "You know that the rulers of the Gentiles lord it over them, and their great men exercise authority over them. It is not this way among you, but whoever wishes to become great among you shall be your servant, and whoever wishes to be first among you shall be your slave; just as the Son of Man did not come to be served, but to serve, and to give His life a ransom for many" (Matthew 20:25-28).

It is out of this bedrock of security, being rooted and grounded in Jesus' love, that we're able to consider the relationship of Jews and Gentiles within the Body of Messiah.

To Understand the Relationship, Romans is Relevant

How should Gentile Christians view Messianic Jews? How should they view themselves in relationship to Messianic Jews? I find Romans to be a prophetic book for our time. The founders of the Roman house-churches were Jewish believers. However, communities of Jesus followers in Rome were growing outside the ethnic boundaries of Israel in exile. Proselytes, God-fearers, their immediate (Gentile) families, extended families and friends were coming into the Kingdom.

Apparently, there was a great deal of disruption in Jewish communities because of the gospel. According to Acts 18:2 and some secular sources, the emperor, Claudius, expelled Rome's Jewish residents. This included the Jewish remnant who were loyal to Jesus. When Claudius died, the ban was lifted and the Roman Messianic Jews returned.

What did they find when they got home? They found that another culture had replaced the initial life-pattern of the church in Rome. The initiating leaders had been exiled. Now they had returned and were meeting new leaders and new disciples of Gentile Roman house churches. Indigenous Gentile leadership had emerged who saw the Scriptures differently, led different lifestyles and had a different view of God and the Messiah. Despite the deeply engrained cultural anti-Semitism of Rome, I'm sure that the Gentile believers were glad their brethren and spiritual fathers had returned. However, differences in spiritual emphases had arisen. Some of these differences were anti-Jewish deviations from the apostolic outlook that may have been rooted in Greco-Roman negative attitudes towards the Jewish people. These caused spiritual, theological and cultural conflicts that Paul addressed in this letter.

This Parallels Our Situation

For practically 1900 years, Jewish believers have been numerically next to non-existent, inconsequential or assimilated into an essentially Gentile Church. Since 1967 there has been a resurgence of Jewish discipleship. It is similar to the Jewish remnant's return to Rome. There are questions about how the Gentile Church should relate to this phenomenon and how they are connected to Israel's remnant. Paul's letter to Roman house churches offers keys to unlock these conundrums. In this letter, God's heart for the Jewish people and the apostolic understanding of Israel's importance is revealed. In Romans, we find instruction about how Jews and Gentiles might develop unity while maintaining distinctive, God given identities. Paul taught them how they were to view, embrace and serve one another.

Within the context of Paul's guidance concerning Jewish-Gentile reconciliation, one reads of a coming greater reconciliation. Paul heralded a restoration of the whole of Israel to their God and Messiah. He took that proclamation further and prophesied that there is a relationship between the deliverance of the Jewish people and the consummation of the ages. Search all you want, there is no better example of this apostolic eschatology in the New Testament. This thorough rehearsal of prophetic truths regarding Israel's restoration and the age-to-come is clearly enunciated in Romans.

In Romans, Paul appealed to Gentile God-lovers to identify with God's heart. He reminded them of the immediate relevance of the already ancient revelation that Father loves the Jewish people for the sake of the patriarchs.

In Romans, Paul appealed to Gentile God-lovers to identify with God's heart.

> ...from the standpoint of God's choice they are beloved for the sake of the fathers (Romans 11:28b).

Paul was the premier apostle to the Gentiles. He opened his heart and exhorted Gentile disciples to view life according to their apostle's perspective. Despite what it may have looked like, he emphatically did not view Israel as a rejected people. Rather, Paul taught they are a people whom God preserves.

> I say then, God has not rejected His people, has He? May it never be! For I too am an Israelite, a descendant

> of Abraham, of the tribe of Benjamin. God has not rejected His people whom He foreknew (Romans 11:1-2a).

Paul saw them as beloved for the sake of the patriarchs. He proclaimed that their chosenness (11:28), gifts and calling (11:29) were permanent.

> From the standpoint of the gospel they are enemies for your sake, but from the standpoint of God's choice they are beloved for the sake of the fathers; for...the gifts and the calling of God are irrevocable (Romans 11:28-29).

He saw the Jewish people as the doorway to the full manifestation of the Kingdom. Paul explicitly taught that his people's restoration was a means to a marvelous end.

> Now if their transgression is riches for the world and their failure is riches for the Gentiles, how much more will their fulfillment be!...For if their rejection is the reconciliation of the world, what will their acceptance be but life from the dead? (Romans 11:12, 15)

Let's review this. Look at Romans 11:12:

> Now if their transgression is riches for the world and their failure is riches for the Gentiles, how much more will their fulfillment be!

Look at this syllogism from Romans 11:12:

- Their transgression = riches for the world
- Their failure = riches for the Gentiles
- Their fulfillment = more riches for the world and more riches for the nations of the world

Here is Romans 11:15:

> For if their rejection is the reconciliation of the world, what will their acceptance be but life from the dead?

From this, Paul calls the readers to accept this logical consequence:

- Their rejection = reconciliation of the cosmos
- Their acceptance = life from the dead

Here is Paul's prophetic perspective: If the Jewish people's failure to receive the Messiah Jesus produces worldwide blessings, then their certain future reconciliation to their King will cause unspeakable, unimaginable blessings to burst forth. Apart from these convictions, there is no Pauline understanding of the end-times and the age-to-come. It was important to Paul. He pled with the Gentile disciples to embrace this. Read his instruction as a plea,

> *Brethren, please receive this and then answer me. What will their acceptance be but life from the dead?*

Paul wanted his Gentile disciples to eagerly anticipate the fulfillment of Israel's hope: the resurrection of the dead and the coming Messianic age. He was willing to pay with his life for the maintenance of this proclamation:

> *There is a coming age. It is what we as a people have always longed for. It is coming. It is the hope of Israel.*

Take some time and look at the consistency of his defense of Israel's hope:

> Paul began crying out in the Council, "Brethren, I am a Pharisee, a son of Pharisees; I am on trial for the hope and resurrection of the dead!" (Acts 23:6b)

> But this I admit to you, that according to the Way which they call a sect I do serve the God of our fathers, believing everything that is in accordance with the Law and that is written in the Prophets; having a hope in God, which these men cherish themselves, that there

> shall certainly be a resurrection of both the righteous and the wicked (Acts 24:14-15).
>
> And now I am standing trial for the hope of the promise made by God to our fathers; the promise to which our twelve tribes hope to attain, as they earnestly serve God night and day. And for this hope, O King, I am being accused by Jews. Why is it considered incredible among you people if God does raise the dead? (Acts 26:6-8)
>
> For this reason, therefore, I requested to see you and to speak with you, for I am wearing this chain for the sake of the hope of Israel (Acts 28:20).

Some Gentile believers in Rome may have been ignorant. Some may have resisted these realities, but Paul prophesied the coming restoration of Israel and the fulfillment of Israel's hope.

> For I do not want you, brethren, to be uninformed of this mystery—so that you will not be wise in your own estimation—that a partial hardening has happened to Israel until the fullness of the Gentiles has come in; and so all Israel will be saved; just as it is written, "THE DELIVERER WILL COME FROM ZION, HE WILL REMOVE UNGODLINESS FROM JACOB. THIS IS MY COVENANT WITH THEM, WHEN I TAKE AWAY THEIR SINS" (Romans 11:25b-27).

These verses reference unbelieving Israel's end-time salvation. They are not cryptic references to a Glorious Gentile Church. These words do not require intellectual contortions and the suspension of the commonly held meanings of words. Just look at the plain verses that come next:

> From the standpoint of the gospel they are enemies for your sake, but from the standpoint of God's choice they are beloved for the sake of the fathers; for the gifts and the calling of God are irrevocable (Romans 11:28-29).

Paul was called to the Gentiles. In response, the Gentile Church is to be distinctively discipled by Paul. His point of view provides a pattern. His identification with God's heart is a window through which all may share the God of Abraham, Isaac, and Jacob's heart for His people, Israel. A disciple who receives this New Testament revelation is enabled to more comprehensively understand his identity and role in relationship to the Church.

Reconciliation to True Identity

Who are you in relationship to the Jewish remnant? How should Gentile Christians view their relationship to Messianic Jews? These chapters are primarily written to Gentile believers who love the Jewish people. To you I restate the obvious, Gentile and Jewish believers in Jesus are spiritual family.

Many see the Church as the continuity, or expansion, of ancient Israel. Yet, apparently, they believe this continuity has no connection to Jewish people. To them, Jews are irrelevant to a true understanding of "the Israel of God." To them, "Israel" no longer carries a connotation of connection to Jewish people. I want to address this, for I believe it will prove beneficial for non-Jews to know how the Bible says they fit in this family.

Many see the Church as the continuity, or expansion, of ancient Israel. Yet, apparently, they believe this continuity has no connection to Jewish people.

How *They* Fit?

Gentile Christians generally don't see this as an issue. They suppose that any Jewish person who believes should fit into the Church as it has existed through the centuries. This is not a Biblical perspective; it is a cultural and demographic anachronism. In Paul's letters, it is the Gentiles who are being fit in. Paul has been read through a skewed lens. Gentile Christians have been emotionally acculturated and taught in a way that comfortably views the Church as being 99.9% non-Jewish. To make Paul's letters relevant to themselves, on their own terms, they understand his letters from that perspective. Many subconsciously presuppose a demographic situation that did not exist when these epistles were written.

Imagine a pie chart divided into two sections. One is white; the other is black. The overwhelming black color on the pie represents Gentiles. A small sliver of white represents the Jewish believers. That is a good representation of the demographics of the Church throughout the millennia.

It may look something like this:

This may be a good demographic representation of the Church over the centuries. However, when the New Testament was written, this was not the case. Apart from the time of John's writings, the demographic composition of the international Body of Messiah was overwhelmingly Jewish.

Imagine the pie chart again. This time imagine that the black part of the pie, representing Messianic Jewish disciples, was 99% Jewish and the 1% of the pie were Gentile believers. Then, over the course of time, perhaps by the time Paul's writings were completed, the Gentile population in the Church had steadily grown. They steadily grew from .5%, to maybe 8%, or perhaps even 12% of what we call the universal Church.

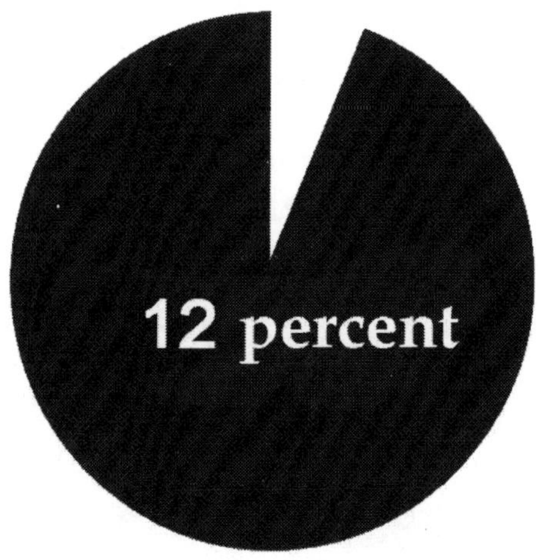

Throughout Paul's ministry, the communities he established experienced remarkable growth amongst the Gentiles. They grew to be Gentile-majority churches. However, the primary ethnic composition of the International Church was Jewish. He addressed the question of Gentile identity in Jesus from the midst of that social and cultural challenge.

It was a shock when Gentiles began to get converted to the one true God through the Messiah. During this theological earthquake, some conflict arose. From what I understand, there was a battle on two fronts. The first, addressed by Paul in his letters, was the fight for the dignity of the Gentile believers. He also addressed how they were to relate to Messianic Jews and the rest of Israel. He stood up for the integrity of the gospel.

> For I am not ashamed of the gospel, for it is the power of God for salvation to everyone who believes, to the Jew first and also to the Greek (Romans 1:16).

At the same time, Jewish believers fought against being marginalized by their own people. They saw themselves as the godly remnant of their nation and self-identified to Roman authorities as being part of Israel, a protected people. The Jewish people did not have to worship the emperor or pay public respect to pagan gods. Jewish believers wanted these rights to continue for themselves and extend to their Gentile converts. One can trace this theme in Acts.

The believers succeeded in the first conflict. The dignity of the Gentile Christian was guarded and blessed. The Church failed in the second. The growing demographic success of the missions to the Gentiles threatened the social structure of Roman society. In reaction, belief in Jesus was denied the status of *religio licita*, permitted religion. Consequently, Jewish and Gentile believers were sporadically persecuted throughout the Roman Empire.

Let's focus upon the first area of conflict because with the rise of Messianic Judaism and the reestablishment of the nation-state Israel, it is relevant to Gentile believers. How should Gentile disciples see themselves? What does the Bible teach?

Let's put ourselves in the demographic shoes of early Gentile believers. Imagine that each preeminent minister of the gospel in the world is Jewish

Let's put ourselves in the demographic shoes of early Gentile believers. Imagine that each preeminent minister of the gospel in the world is Jewish and that they minister amongst other Jewish people. Let's give this a try...

- Billy Graham? He's Jewish and lives in Boca Raton.
- Bill Bright? A Jew from Philadelphia.
- The Pope? Jewish, from Manhattan.
- C. S. Lewis? Also, a Jew, from the Hamptons.

- Oral Roberts? A former Hasidic rabbi from Boston.

In this fictional universe, if they have a recognizable name in the Body of Christ, they are Jewish believers.

In fact, Messianic Jewish believers run every seminary. All the seminarians are Messianic Jews. Furthermore, every Christian publishing company, magazine, website, worship leader or major media ministry is run by Messianic Jewish believers. They all carry Messianic Jewish resources. There are millions of them. They pray in Hebrew, keep kosher, honor the Sabbath, etc.

And then, suddenly, out of the blue, somewhere in Minnesota, there is a people movement amongst some Scandinavians. Let's make believe this is a spiritual explosion and that 50,000 of them have come to the Lord in the last few months.

The leaders who brought the gospel to Minnesota are Jews from Brooklyn named Saul and Jacob (who travel with a couple of Italian proselytes). They demonstrated the power of God and discipled these new believers into communities. These Minnesotans renounced their worship of Thor and are loyal to the God of Abraham, Isaac, and Jacob. They believe that the God of Israel became incarnate in a Jewish man, Yeshua, who was born in Borough Park and ministered in Manhattan. They trust that He was crucified, entombed and raised from the dead in Central Park. The Scriptures they now study are about the history of the Jewish people's interaction with their God.

After the immediate joy of meeting God through Jesus, they begin to ask...

Wait a second, this whole thing is Jewish...

How do I fit in?

They look for counsel...

> *One of my neighbors, Alvin Borg, visited some churches in Manhattan. Al was told he must assimilate to become a follower of Jesus in good standing. At first, he rejected this, but Borg's resistance was futile. He went through a conversion process, received circumcision and Alvin now tells me I have to do the same thing for the Messiah's sacrifice to be effectual in my life. Is this right?*

Imagine the social pressure. Imagine the spiritual insecurity. Imagine the theological confusion. Think of the ethnic alienation, pride and resentment. This was the social situation of Paul's Gentile converts.

Something like this happened...

In Acts 15 the apostles and elders of the international Church met in Jerusalem to settle the problem of how they should relate to Gentiles who believed in Jesus. There were no non-Jewish representatives at this council. This reflected the demographics of the universal Church. Consider the following:

The twelve apostles were Jewish,

> "that is, Peter and John and James and Andrew, Philip and Thomas, Bartholomew and Matthew, James the son of Alphaeus, and Simon the Zealot, and Judas the son of James" (Acts 1:13).

The half-brother of the Messiah, the chief leader in Jerusalem, James (Jacob), was Jewish. The foundational members of the churches throughout the Empire were Jewish believers who most likely had their roots in Jerusalem. The only evangelist named in the New Testament, Philip, was a Hellenic Jew. Philip's daughters were Jewish prophetesses.

The first martyr, Stephen, was a Hellenic Jew who had a ministry marked by signs and wonders. The leader of the primary itinerate prophetic company, Agabus, was Jewish. Paul, Barnabas, Silas, Apollos, John Mark and Timothy were the primary missionaries to the Gentiles and they were

Messianic Jews. Who are the primary non-Jewish participants mentioned in Acts? Luke (most likely), Titus and Trophimus.

Let's reimagine that pie chart. This time the chart represents the ethnic backgrounds of the Church's leadership. The over-

whelming black 99% of the chart is comprised of Jewish apostles and elders. there is a sliver of white indicating leaders who were non-Jewish.

In the light of these demographics it is not unlikely that sincere Gentile believers may have had questions about their relationship to God's people. Questions like...

> *Where do I fit in?*
>
> *Do I have to become Jewish?*
>
> *Must I attach myself to the ethnic people of Israel to be a fully received participant in the life of the Messiah?*
>
> *What is my identity?*

In considering this, we will discover and celebrate Paul's guidance. With his supervision, we will see principles of how to build unity between Gentile Christians and today's Messianic Jews.

2
Paul's Example

PAUL HAD BEEN TAUGHT TO GUARD THE DIGNITY OF Gentiles, which he did as seen in his epistles. To understand this, we need to see that the two primary schools of Pharisees were led by opposing sages, Hillel and Shammai. They disagreed about many things. For instance, Hillel taught that divorce was permissible for the mildest offense. Shammai taught that divorce was not permitted. Does that sound familiar? The gospels record that sometimes Rabbi Jesus was asked to weigh in on these disputes. One issue over which these Pharisaic schools had a controversy was the status of Gentiles in the age-to-come.

Shammai taught that the coming age was for the Jewish people. Period. If a non-Jew was to participate in the Messianic Kingdom, they needed to become Jews. In addition, Shammai's followers discouraged the conversion of Gentiles.

Hillel disagreed. He taught that righteous Gentiles should maintain their status as Gentiles and would participate in the coming age as Gentiles. However, if a Gentile wanted to become part of Israel this Pharisaic movement would welcome them.

Paul was discipled by Hillel's grandson, Gamaliel.

> I am a Jew, born in Tarsus of Cilicia, but brought up in this city, educated under Gamaliel (Acts 22:3a).

In the early Church, there was a controversy along these lines. Those called "Judaizers" believed a non-Jew must convert and become a Jew for the blood of Jesus to be effectual. Most likely, these believing Pharisees were influenced by Shammai.

Paul, a believing Pharisee, discipled by Gamaliel the grandson of Hillel, stood against that heresy. You can read about it at length in Galatians. In another epistle, he revealed that Gentile believers did not have to become Jews. However, Jewish believers should welcome Gentile disciples as fellow citizens of the Kingdom. Why? Because God welcomed them. For Paul, the current age represented and foreshadowed the fullness of the coming Messianic Kingdom. In that Kingdom, the nations, as nations, are loyal to both Israel's Messiah and Israel's godly remnant, the Jewish apostolic movement.

> So then you (Gentiles) are no longer strangers and aliens, but you (Gentiles) are fellow citizens with the saints (the holy Remnant of Israel), and are of God's household, having been built on the foundation of the (Jewish) apostles and (the Remnant of Israel's) prophets, Messiah Jesus Himself being the cornerstone (Ephesians 2:19-20).

Please read this abridged section of Ephesians in the light of this controversy between Paul, the rabbi apostle schooled by Gamaliel, and the "Judaizers," spiritual offspring of Shammai.

> Therefore, remember that formerly you, the Gentiles in the flesh...remember that you were at that time separate from the Messiah, excluded from the commonwealth of Israel, and strangers to the covenants of promise, having no hope and without God in the world. But now in the Messiah Jesus you who formerly were far off have been brought near by the blood of the Messiah... So then you are no longer strangers and aliens, but you are fellow citizens with the saints, and are of God's household (Ephesians 2:11a-13, 19).

The Jesus-believing Gentiles asked, "How do I fit in?" Some replied, "You are not welcome unless you become Jewish." But Paul had the Messiah's mind on this matter. He said, in effect,

> *You are welcome as you are.*

> *You do not have to become ethnically Jewish and follow Torah like we do. If you believe in Jesus, you have been brought near to God through the Messiah's blood.*
>
> *Do you want to know your status?*
>
> *You are no longer strangers and aliens. You are fellow citizens of His Kingdom together with the saints, the Messianic Jewish remnant.*

Fellow Citizens

Where did he get this idea? Paul may have reached into his own experience to express this spiritual reality. He was a citizen of Tarsus, Rome and Heaven.

Tarsus:

> But Paul said, "I am a Jew of Tarsus in Cilicia, a CITIZEN of no insignificant city" (Acts 21:39a, emphasis mine).

Rome:

> The commander came and said to him, "Tell me, are you a Roman?" And he said, "Yes." The commander answered, "I acquired this CITIZENSHIP with a large sum of money." And Paul said, "But I was actually born a CITIZEN" (Acts 22:27-28, emphasis mine).

Heaven:

> For our CITIZENSHIP is in heaven (Philippians 3:20a, emphasis mine).

Let's focus upon Paul's Roman citizenship. Paul was not ethnically a Latin, but he was a Roman. Citizenship in the Empire was not just relegated to ethnicity, but to loyalty and value. People could earn citizenship. People could purchase citizenship. Often, retired Roman soldiers would be rewarded with citizenship. Citizens had rights, responsibilities and privileges. Paul was not an Italian Roman, but he had the rights, responsibilities and privileges of someone who was an ethnically Roman citizen. Paul was a Roman citizen from birth.

The Gentile believers were not born Jews. They were not part of the holy remnant of ethnic Israel. However, they were now fellow citizens with the saints. They were born again into this Kingdom relationship. This is a big concept.

Remember, at the time this was written, perhaps 10-15% of the universal Church were Gentiles. The primary leadership of the Church—apostles, prophets, evangelists, pastors and teachers—were Messianic Jews. The overwhelming majority of the international Body were Jewish. Paul referred to them as "the saints" (holy ones). All the promises, covenants, and eschatological hopes of Israel rightly resided with the remnant. Israel's godly remnant represented the entire people and had a New Covenant relationship with God. These holy ones (saints, the godly Remnant) were in relationship with the Messiah. They had received the down payment of the Spirit and therefore had the certain hope of participation in the future age. How blessed they were.

And now, beyond expectation, astonishingly, these Gentiles are part of that number. They are connected to the Messiah; they partake of His Kingdom and the heritage of Israel. They are no longer strangers to the covenants of promise; they are welcomed members of the family. They have a confident expectation of eternal life and, in this dark cosmos, they have a relationship with the God of Israel. They are connected to the Messianic Jewish believers, the priestly remnant representatives of Israel. They are "fellow citizens."

Realignment by Faith

There is order inherent in relationships. Look what Paul wrote in Ephesians. He revealed that believing Gentiles were spiritually connected to the Messiah and, though a small minority in the universal Body, find their identity in full identification with the Messianic Jewish remnant (Ephesians 2:11a-13,19).

He taught the same thing in a different way through the metaphor of the olive tree and its branches:

> But if some of the branches (*majority-Israel*) were broken off, and you (*Gentiles*), being a wild olive, were grafted in among them (*the Messianic Jewish believers*) and became partaker with them (the Messianic Jewish believers) of the rich (*Jewish*) root of the olive tree, do not be arrogant toward the branches (*the Messianic Jewish believers*); but if you are arrogant, remember that it is not you who supports the (*Jewish*) root, but the (*Jewish*) root supports you (*Gentile believers*) (Romans 11:17-18, clarifications mine).

This small percentage of true, highly valued, blood purchased believers from the nations, was grafted in among the super majority of Messianic Jewish believers. If the Gentile believers were able to receive the revelation of the value and extraordinary destiny of the Messianic Jewish remnant, they would rejoice in the privilege of being connected to the olive tree, in among them, partaking of the root of Israel's patriarchs.

Obviously, historically, this has not been the case. However, it is the biblical reality. Let's allow the Bible to determine our vision. To that end, remember that at the end of Romans, Paul urged Jewish and Gentile believers to receive one another.

> Therefore, accept one another, just as the Messiah also accepted us to the glory of God (Romans 15:7).

Then the apostle enjoined true believers from the nations to join Israel's remnant in worship of the one true God. As they do, they demonstrate the reality of the coming Kingdom's full manifestation.

> Again he says, "REJOICE, O GENTILES, WITH HIS PEOPLE" (Romans 15:10).

To this day, according to the Apostolic Writings, believers from the nations are "with" His people, the remnant of Israel. Received by God, they worship together.

Paul was sent to the nations and welcomed those who responded to the gospel. He saw them as fellow citizens with the saints, grafted in among the Jewish believers. The King totally received them and the Jewish believers were called to "accept" those their King received. However, when Paul said that the Gentiles are "with" God's people, he preserved a sense of order. His intention was to prevent their potential arrogance. His warning was ignored. However, this hubris is now being put right.

> *When Paul said that the Gentiles are "with" God's people, he preserved a sense of order. His intention was to prevent their potential arrogance.*

When one looks at the demographics over the history of the Church, one must search to find hints of the "natural branches." This is true to this day. It looks like a Gentile institution until one looks at the nature of the tree. It is a Jewish tree. It is "their own olive tree." The tree belongs to the Jewish people.

> ...God is able to graft them in again. For if you were cut off from what is by nature a wild olive tree, and were grafted contrary to nature into a cultivated olive tree, how much more will these who are the natural branches be grafted into their own olive tree? (Romans 11:23c-24)

Consider the quantity of Gentile disciples compared to the number of Jewish believers. If numbers are the deciding factor, then Jewish believers are being grafted in among the Gentile branches in a newly reconstituted olive tree comprised of redeemed Gentiles. However, let's look at something different than numbers. Consider the weight of these believers.

Here's what I mean: If you had to choose one or the other, what would you do? Would you rather be associated with every Gentile Christian evangelist who ever lived, or the Messianic Jew, Peter? Would you choose to be taught by all the Gentile Christian teachers who ever lived, or the Messianic Rabbi, Paul? Would you rather receive revelation from all the Gentile Christian prophets who ever lived, or the Messianic Jewish seer, John?

Would you prefer to participate in every historic Holy Spirit revival amongst the nations, or with the initial outpouring of the Spirit on Shavuot, Pentecost, upon the Messianic Jewish believers in Jerusalem? Would you rather receive the witness of every Gentile believer who ever lived, or the Messianic Jewish witnesses of Jesus' resurrection? Whose witness is more authoritative? Would you wish to experience the discipling dynamic of all the Gentile communities of believers that have ever been established, or participate in the Messianic Jewish believing community in Jerusalem (Acts 2-4)?

So, who is to line up with whom? What is the Biblical worldview? How should identity and priorities be decided? Upon what basis?

Kavod: glory, or weightiness

I would like to suggest two ways of comparison. One is numeric, the other is weight. Numerically, one would judge that Jewish believers should line up with the Gentile Church. However, the comparative weight seems to indicate that the reverse is the case and is, in fact, the reality of what is happening.

With whom would all the Gentile evangelists, teachers, and prophets who have lived throughout the centuries want to be in relationship? They would choose the twelve original apostles,

Paul, their practice, doctrine, experience, and the communities they established.

Biblically, the whole Gentile membership of the universal Church should see themselves according to the Pauline epistles. They are called to see themselves as fellow citizens together with, grafted in among, the remnant of Israel.

Prophetic, Intercessory Order

I have a suggestion for those who have read this and are being drawn to a fresh appraisal of their holy identity. By a revolutionary faith, identify with the biblical narrative, not Church history.

If you agree, declare the following:

- I see myself in relationship to Israel as I was instructed by the Apostle to the Gentiles.
- Despite the overwhelming majority of Gentile believers, I identify myself in reference to the Jewish remnant.
- It is their olive tree. I am grafted in among them in their own olive tree.
- I am a fully enfranchised citizen together with, and in connection to, these saints.
- As a friend of God, I am loyal to the Messiah of Israel and the holy remnant of Israel who are part of the people of Israel.
- As someone who is a friend of God, I identify with His love for these people for the sake of His love for the patriarchs.

- As a priest of God, I identify in prayer with the Jewish people and seek God concerning their salvation and wellbeing.
- I look forward to the day when these prayers are answered and there will be life from the dead.

Summation:

Part of the hatred between nations and ethnic groups is founded upon the rejection of God's authority. The nations are called to inherit a blessing through blessing Israel, God's first-born son.

> And I will bless those who bless you, and the one who curses you I will curse. And in you all the families of the earth will be blessed (Genesis 12:3).

When the nations unite in blessing Israel, putting away their hatred of another's "chosenness," they will learn to honor each other as well. The difficult task of honoring Israel, God's choice, provides the pattern for the nations' mutual honor. When will this transformation from mutual hatred to mutual honor happen? It is happening now, in the Church.

Begin. Honor the God who chooses. Line up with Genesis 12:3 and practice relating to people of other nations by decreeing blessing upon His firstborn nation-son. When you bless Israel, you learn how to bless others. When you bless Israel, you come in on the blessing, for God blesses those who bless them. And now, by the way, you are grafted in among them. As you do, recognize this ancient word as relevant:

Honor the God who chooses. Line up with Genesis 12:3 and practice relating to people of other nations by decreeing blessing upon His firstborn nation-son.

> For thus says the LORD of hosts, "After glory He has sent me against the nations which plunder you, for he who touches you, touches the apple of His eye" (Zechariah 2:8).

Yes, the pupil of the eye is sensitive. Another aspect of the "apple of His eye" is that God sees things through the lens of their wellbeing.

See with God's eyes.

3

God's Unique Love for Israel

THERE IS NO REASON FOR ANY GENTILE TO SEEK significance through adapting a pseudo-Jewish identity. The measure of how God values every person is Calvary (Romans 5:8). The price at which we're assessed is staggering.

> You were not redeemed with perishable things like silver or gold from your futile way of life inherited from your forefathers, but with precious blood, as of a lamb unblemished and spotless, the blood of the Messiah (1 Peter 1:18-19).

Each person is more than significant. Everyone should be encouraged to step into this reality:

> The life which I now live in the flesh I live by faith in the Son of God, who loved me and gave Himself up for me (Galatians 2:20b).

I am not going to footnote this because the list is too long. Let it be established that every believer (Jew and Gentile) is incorporated into the life of Jesus, one spirit with the Lord. We may describe this as participation in the Messiah's Body, or God's Olive Tree, or the True Vine, or the transnational Priesthood, or Wife, or Bride, or Temple, or Commonwealth of Israel, etc. Every believer (Jew and Gentile) is justified the same way, sanctified by the presence of God's Spirit and will be glorified in the Resurrection of the Righteous. Every disciple (Jew and Gentile) is growing in the fruit of the same Spirit, being equipped to serve, and has the same Commission.

The favor of Jesus, the Father's affection and the fellowship of the Holy Spirit are the immediate experience of Jesus' followers

(Jew and Gentile). Jewish and Gentile believers are heirs together, friends forever, one new man in Jesus. The Scriptures are treasured by each disciple (Jew and Gentile) and guide our common faith.

They have access by the same Spirit to the same Father through the same Messiah and worship the same God. They have the sum of all spiritual riches in the heavenlies, and... the list can go on and on. Paul wrote:

> There is one body and one Spirit, just as also you were called in one hope of your calling; one Lord, one faith, one baptism, one God and Father of all who is over all and through all and in all (Ephesians 4:4-6).

The believer's status in the Kingdom of Heaven is amazing. The power of God working toward those who believe is overwhelming. The spiritual authority in the Name of Jesus is a common stewardship. In Jesus, there is no male, female, Jew, Gentile, rich, poor, educated, ignorant. There is a remarkable unity in the Body of the Messiah. Redeemed Jews and Gentiles share a common destiny in Him.

Distinctions

Even in the light of these aforementioned realities, the Scriptures testify to the distinct callings of Israel and the Nations. Many believers have a hard time reconciling these realities and I've been asked,

> *The Scriptures testify to the distinct callings of Israel and the Nations. Many believers have a hard time reconciling these realities.*

- Does God love Israel more than other nations?
- Does He love individual Jews, because they're Jewish, more than individual Gentiles?

Sometimes these inquiries come from sincere seekers. At other times the questions are "gotcha," belligerent, angry challenges from offended Gentile Christians. Usually those who ask apparently think these questions mean the same thing. They don't.

I don't recall hearing these questions from Jewish believers. Those I know take for granted that God loves all individuals enough to incarnate and die for them. The preeminent Messianic Jewish Apostle to the Gentiles wrote:

> For we maintain that a man is justified by faith apart from works of the Law. Or is God the God of Jews only? Is He not the God of Gentiles also? Yes, of Gentiles also, since indeed God who will justify the circumcised by faith and the uncircumcised through faith is one (Romans 3:28-30).

Still, these are two serious questions that deserve sincere answers. To me, the first inquiry has to do with God's eschatological, geopolitical economy. The second is about the relative worth of individuals. We may legitimately ask if there is a difference between the types of love He has for individuals and nations. Are these "loves" the same? Does He love nations in the same way, and for the same reasons, He loves people? Is there a difference? Recognizing some of my limitations, I'll try to provide an explanation.

What leads to these questions?

Why are these questions asked? Let's begin with some history. It is a historical fact that the predominantly Gentile Church has been arrogant towards the Jewish people. In addition, this same Church has been the primary source of the persecution of Israel in exile.[1]

Look at the indictment of Israel's King:

> I was hungry, and you gave Me nothing to eat; I was thirsty, and you gave Me nothing to drink; I was a

> stranger, and you did not invite Me in; naked, and you did not clothe Me; sick, and in prison, and you did not visit Me (Matthew 25:42-43).

Examine the history of the Diaspora (the scattering of the Jewish people).

Can it be said that the Church nourished, showed hospitality, clothed, and comforted the Jewish people? No, the Church did the opposite. It provided a theological framework that encouraged "Christian" governments to rob them of the right to derive a livelihood through certain occupations. Rather than welcome, the Church encouraged nations to expel them (repeated "ethnic cleansing"). Rather than clothe, they stripped. Rather than comfort they, harassed. Rather than protect, they plundered. It was upon the basis of supersessionism (Replacement Theology) that the Nazi regime flourished.

Less malign, but spiritually injurious, is this: year in and year out, teachers of the Church use the Jewish people[2] as foils to illustrate sin, self-righteousness, judgmentalism, idolatry, insincere liturgy, and self-absorption in contrast with holiness, righteousness, mercy, true worship, and love. Having separated the prophets and apostles from their people, the Church uses Israel's oracles (which includes the New Testament) to hold the Jewish people up to scorn and bolster their own self-image.

To those who hubristically hated the Jewish people and ignored the apostle Paul's injunction to adjure arrogance,[3] it is possible that the Spirit may say this:

> What right have you to tell of My statutes and to take My covenant in your mouth? (Psalm 50:16b)

They had no right. They have no right, nor will they ever have authentic spiritual authority to preach the Scriptures in a way that undermines God's purposes and distorts His heart. Yet, for centuries the Church derided the Jewish people as "Christ-killers" and denounced them as "Deicides." The Church taught that God concluded His covenant with Israel and replaced Israel with itself. This is theological anti-Semitism. It is alien to God's heart and foreign to the message of His prophets and apostles.

The culture of the historic churches is theologically anti-Semitic. Their ecclesiology encouraged ethnic anti-Semitism. But now believers are being exposed to what the Bible says: God loves the Jewish people. They are discovering sacred apostolic themes that are surprisingly different than these age-long presuppositions.

The culture of the historic churches is theologically anti-Semitic. But now believers are being exposed to what the Bible says: God loves the Jewish people.

No wonder these questions are being asked.

Roots

> Sir, did you not sow good seed in your field? How then does it have tares? (Matthew 13:27b)

In Matthew 13:38 "the field is the world." However, the Church is also called, "God's field" (1 Corinthians 3:9). The Messiah of Israel sowed good seed in that field. In parallel to the parable of the tares, the enemy has sown seeds that threaten the nature of the field (of the Church) and the quality of the harvest. These supersessionist seeds were received by the field and put down roots. They grew and produced fruit that filled the Church and affected the nations' attitudes and actions towards the Jewish people.

> ...a root bearing poisonous fruit and wormwood (Deuteronomy 29:18c).

How deep and wide are the roots of this deception? What fruit has been borne? Consider this: what will happen if these roots are exposed and removed? After all, roots provide stability and nourishment. What do these roots stabilize? What do they nurture? This cunning doctrine has provided a false persona that has been eagerly embraced and disseminated. It has marked much of the Church's mission. When these roots are extricated, the structures and proclamation of the Church are affected.

It is wonderful that so much of the Church's activity has been redemptive, but it is only a shadow of what God has in store. Here's a principle: God exalts the humble and humbles those who exalt themselves (1 Peter 5:5). Can you imagine the glory that will come upon and be revealed through the Church when they honor God's heart towards Israel? Why, it may be enough to fulfill Paul's hope and provoke the Jewish people to jealousy![4]

What kind of work must be done to excise these rot-spreading diseased doctrines? It takes consistent instruction. It takes courage to compassionately confront, care that stirs prayer and concern that motivates spiritual warfare. It requires a resilient, thorough reworking of spiritual-theological presuppositions. This demonic spiritual heritage must be uprooted by the power of the Holy Spirit through the application of the Scriptures, penitent prayer, authoritative renunciation and restitution. These teachings, unchallenged for practically two millennia, have shaped the self-understanding of the Church. Truth that brings humility produces better fruit than the lies that manifest and encourage pride.

Hatred and pride are addictive and contagious. It is hard to give up these attitudes and replace them with love and humility. It takes holy, love-filled laborers who have a vision for the fullness of the Church and the restoration of Israel. And people are working towards this end.

Many Christian teachers are applying themselves to this goal. The emphases upon God's calling of Israel, His love and His purposes are being consistently heralded. There are now generations of believers who have been raised with a baseline doctrinal understanding that "God is not finished with the Jews." This is good, as far as it goes. At this time, God is granting greater insight into the Scriptures. He is building upon that foundation. Why? He is revealing His heart for the purpose of prayerful and practical intercession on behalf of His people.

The whole process has been a bit disorienting. There are extremes expressed by some whose brand of Christian Zionism has embraced dual-covenant theology. Others have promoted strange innovations that have their root in British-Israelism. Others seek to make "Torah Observance" mandatory for Gentiles. It is no surprise that in the confusing mix of legitimately changing paradigms and heretical exaggerations there are reactionaries who cling to supersessionism. And then there are some who simply hate the truth. It is not surprising that these questions arise.

God is revealing His heart for the purpose of prayerful and practical intercession on behalf of His people.

Some don't want to get it.

There are those who, upon being exposed to Biblical truths concerning the Jewish people, respond adversely. Some were not raised with anything resembling the full counsel of God concerning Israel and God's heart. Perhaps teachers who spread supersessionism influenced them. On the other hand, some fervently espoused classical Dispensationalism and expected a pre-tribulation rapture to happen. The dates passed and their disillusionment provoked an overreaction as the disenchanted rejected the prophecies concerning Israel and the Jewish people's restoration. There are those who embrace a leftist narrative of Israel and hate Biblical texts that speak of God's love for Israel as much as they hate the Jewish state. When people like this consider that He might still love Israel "for the sake of the patriarchs" (Romans 11:28b), some tend to get defensive, even overwrought. The way they react is ironically similar to someone who feels as if they are being rejected and "replaced."

In the light of all this, it should not surprise us that there are those who wonder about, or challenge, the nature of God's love for Israel. In comparison to the last couple of thousand years, God's love for the Jewish people is a relatively recent popular emphasis. It calls for a significant reevaluation and readjustment of trans-generational Christian theology and culture. This is not a light matter. How the Church views Israel affects the way it perceives itself, understands God's activity, and frames its hope for the coming ages. This influences the church's spiritual life in foundational ways: worship, intercession, mission priorities, and civic advocacy. It touches upon their conception of God, changes the way they read the Scriptures, and affects their application of the Scriptures.

> *How the Church views Israel affects the way it perceives itself, understands God's activity, and frames its hope for the coming age.*

Change is resisted. It is no surprise that Biblical truths concerning God's love for the Jewish people are often belligerently, defensively contested.

No wonder these questions arise.

What's in a word?

It is possible to understand the aspect of the gospel that pertains to individual salvation and misunderstand the message when it comes to areas of discipleship and expectation.

> I testify to everyone who hears the words of the prophecy of this book: if anyone adds to them, God will add to him the plagues which are written in this book; and if anyone takes away from the words of the book of this prophecy, God will take away his part from the tree of life and from the holy city, which are written in this book (Revelation 22:18-19).

We were specifically warned to neither add nor take away from the inspired words of the Apocalypse.[5] Herein is a principle: for the sake of one's spiritual wellbeing, do not distort the content of God's intended message.[6]

The Church has been careful to preserve the syllables. However, when it comes to God's heart for the Jewish people, the Church has redefined sacred oracles as it seemed suitable. The veneer remained intact; the substance was changed. While stewarding the words they have, perhaps without malicious intent, added to and subtracted from their meaning. A spiritual malaise resulted which can be seen in the spiritual and emotional alienation of the Church from Paul's motivation.

> But I am speaking to you who are Gentiles. Inasmuch then as I am an apostle of Gentiles, I magnify my ministry, if somehow I might move to jealousy my fellow countrymen and save some of them (Romans 11:13-14).

The judgments of the Church towards Israel have been sown and reaped by a Church that does not know its true spiritual condition (Rev. 3:17). There has been a lot of time spent deconstructing Replacement Theology and a commensurate effort seeking to restructure an apostolic Jewish biblical worldview. Why this effort? Because the biblical worldview does not come naturally. How easy might it be for those with demonically enhanced, transgenerational, ethnic anti-Semitic heritages to lapse into theological anti-Semitism? Easy. In addition, societal pressure on believers to disavow any eschatology which in its geopolitical aspects is Israel-concentric is mounting. Therefore, proclamation, prayer and spiritual warfare concerning this is rising up.

> For thus says the LORD, "Sing aloud with gladness for Jacob, and shout among the chief of the nations; Proclaim, give praise and say, 'O LORD, save Your people, the remnant of Israel'" (Jeremiah 31:7).

No wonder these questions arise.

"Yes, or no?"
Framing an Answer:

There is an equivalent of political correctness in the Body. Because of the risk of offending people (or wounding their sense of self-worth) certain issues are avoided or explained away. Seriously, the truth may be painful, but may God forbid that we unnecessarily hurt anyone. May He also help those of us who easily take umbrage.

Believe it or not, there is a tendency to teach so as to please people (Galatians 1:10). Here's a verse that encourages us to have a different motivation:

> Be diligent to present yourself approved to God as a workman who does not need to be ashamed, accurately handling the word of truth (2 Timothy 2:15).

"Accurately handling" comes from a word that means, "cutting a straight path through difficult terrain."[7] This is difficult terrain. How might one do justice to these questions? Let's begin to answer by dealing with this question: "Are individual Jews loved more than individual Gentiles because they are Jews?"

For clarity's sake, let me state that every person on the planet is loved by the Father. All share the common foundation of God's love which measure is the cross.

> But God demonstrates His own love toward us, in that while we were yet sinners, Christ died for us. (Romans 5:8)

Everybody is loved to the degree that the Creator's Son would incarnate and offer Himself up to bring us to Father.

> For Christ also died for sins once for all, the just for the unjust, so that He might bring us to God (1 Peter 3:18a).

The text does not read:

> *For God so loved ISRAEL that He gave His only Son*

He loves humanity and whoever believes on Jesus will have eternal life. God wants each person to be with Him forever.

However, God does not just love individuals. He loves nations comprised of relationships and specific loyalties in which these beloved individuals participate. It has been consistently reiterated in the biblical record that there are divine priorities in the outworking of His geopolitical love. In the midst of the revelation that God loves all nations, the Scriptures convincingly communicate that He values Israel in a unique way. Despite the fact that His love for Israel is a pattern of God's love for all nations, the revelation of this "chosenness" is often found to be troublesome, strange, and offensive (even repulsive) to many Jews and non-Jews, alike.

At the risk of inciting indignation, let's soberly read an outrageous oracle from Isaiah:

> For I am the LORD your God, The Holy One of Israel, your Savior; I have given Egypt as your ransom, Cush and Seba in your place. Since you are precious in My sight, since you are honored and I love you, I will give other men in your place and other peoples in exchange for your life (Isaiah 43:3-4).

Grieved, and maybe envious, many declare this election is unfair. However, I've never heard a believer complain about God's partiality when it is applied to their own life:

> A thousand may fall at your side and ten thousand at your right hand, but it shall not approach you (Psalm 91:7).

Like it or hate it, the prophets specifically speak of God's unique relationship to Israel. There are explicit covenant promises given, dreadful covenant warnings declared and a detailed destiny divinely determined for the Jewish people.

The promise oracles are wonderful, hope-filled and almost too good to be true. Supersessionists want to replace the original recipients of these revelations with themselves apart from any current connection to the Jewish people.

On the other hand, the warnings and denunciations are often too horrible to contemplate, let alone experience.[8] I'm sure there are some supersessionists who believe this aspect of the Mosaic covenant is obsolete together with the people of Israel's election. However, I don't think I've encountered them. Those I've met tend to trumpet their triumphalism on the rubble of the Second Temple and the Diaspora (Luke 21:5-24). I'd be more convinced of the earnest nature of their convictions if those who believe "Israel is the Church" would enthusiastically apply Israel's judgment oracles in the same exclusive manner they lay claim to the Jewish people's irrevocable promises and covenants (Romans 9:3-5; 11:29).

However, in the light of the significant prophecies of promise, it is not unreasonable to inquire along these lines: Does God have a special love for Israel? Does He love this nation more than others?

At times people demand a "yes, or no" answer and refuse to receive anything else. It is like the worn-out joke, "Answer me, yes, or no. Have you stopped beating your spouse yet?" No compliant response can be given that doesn't indict the responder.

Two Mysteries

However, things are not always black and white, yes or no. We must be prepared for nuanced truth if the truth is more complex than the simple answer for which we might hope.

"Nuanced truth" does not mean truth-explained-away, truth-modified so that it becomes a half-truth or a fancy way of framing a falsehood. It does mean that things are not always simple and when we explore mysteries, we may find out they are considered "mysterious" for a reason. Reality is often complicated and the Bible, with its revelations about ultimate reality, is often complicated, too.

In Paul's day, the inclusion of Gentile disciples into the spiritual-socio-political fabric of Israel's commonwealth (represented by Israel's remnant) was a "mystery."[9] Over the last few centuries the biblical truth of the Jewish people's ongoing election has begun to be revisited by the Church. Paul classified this reality as another "mystery". He wrote:

> For I do not want you, brethren, to be uninformed of this mystery—so that you will not be wise in your own estimation—that a partial hardening has happened to Israel until the fullness of the Gentiles has come in; and so all Israel will be saved; just as it is written, "THE DELIVERER WILL COME FROM ZION, HE WILL REMOVE UNGODLINESS FROM JACOB" (Romans 11:25-26).

So, does God love the Jewish people more than other peoples? Yes, or no? My desire is to say that God loves every nation the same exact way. However, despite my culturally formed inclinations, I am forced to answer, "both." Out of His love, God deals with Israel and the nations differently. Both the future glory and the historic outpouring of wrath are uniquely, specifically, revealed and detailed concerning Israel. On the other hand, future glory and judgment are not unique to Israel. God will judge all nations and God will bless the nations. Let's look at some scriptural examples of this in the next chapter.

> *Out of His love,*
> *God deals with Israel*
> *and the nations differently.*

4

God's Love for Other Nations

The prophets of Israel did not just speak to their nation.

God's love for the nations surrounding Israel, even nations that have horrific judgments decreed against them, may be seen in the Scriptures. An example of this is Jeremiah's inspired oracle against Moab and the surprising revelation of God's heartbreak on their behalf. When you read the following summary, you'll find that Moab's judgment follows the pattern found in prophetic denunciations of the Jewish people.

Moab: An Example from Jeremiah 48

In Amos 2:1-2 the prophet foretold coming judgment upon Moab, not because of Moab's actions or attitudes towards Judah or Israel, but because of their cruel disrespect towards Edom. (Think about that!) Centuries later, in the context of Judah's Babylonian captivity, God was still consumed with Moab's wickedness and spoke His mind through Jeremiah. Jeremiah revealed the strategic goals of Moab's enemies. He said that God was crying out to Moab to flee and save their lives. The LORD denounced and judged their false god and decreed the diaspora of their priests and princes (48:1-7).

Moab's cities were divinely destined for destruction. A curse was pronounced upon any of their enemies that did not zealously wage what seems to be described as a genocidal war against Moab. This oracle is in stark contrast to Moab's history that was one of complacency and peace. The LORD said that their judgment would be analogous to the Northern Kingdom's (Israel's) judgment (48:8-13). Moab's military might and confidence is prophetically mocked and their doom is secured. In fact, their disaster would come swiftly (48:14-16).

What was the prophetic exhortation to Moab's neighbors? They were enjoined to mourn, marvel, decree judgment, and inquire. The exhortation was, "Wail and cry out" concerning Moab's destruction (48:17-20).

Part of this overwhelming judgment was due to their hatred and mockery of the Jewish people. They were filled with pride and would pay the price. Their power and the boastful pride of their prowess resulted in their demise (48:21-30) What was God's response to their coming calamity? He wept. He wailed (48:31-32a). His emotions mirrored the prophetic exhortation to Moab itself (48:17, 20).

The judgment oracle continued...

The LORD determined that they would be ruined economically and in every other way. He said, "I will make an end of Moab" (48:35a). Because of this, the prophecy continued, "My (God's) heart wails for Moab like flutes" (48:36a).

The judgment on the people is described.

> "On all the housetops of Moab and in its streets, there is lamentation everywhere; for I have broken Moab like an undesirable vessel," declares the LORD. "How shattered it is! How they have wailed! How Moab has turned his back-- he is ashamed! So Moab will become a laughingstock and an object of terror to all around him" (Jeremiah 48:38-39).

The ultimate verdict contains the summation of Moab's problem. Why are they so evil? Why must they be judged? What is the core issue? Moab will be destroyed from being a people because "he" has become arrogant toward the LORD. (Jeremiah 48:42)

Jeremiah reiterated the archetypical judgment prophesied over the entire planet in Isaiah and applied it to Moab. Moab's doom is a foreshadowing of God's universal wrath, "terror and pit and snare..."

Isaiah wrote:

> Terror and pit and snare confront you, O inhabitant of the earth. Then it will be that he who flees the report of disaster will fall into the pit, and he who climbs out of the pit will be caught in the snare; for the windows above are opened, and the foundations of the earth shake. The earth is broken asunder, the earth is split through, the earth is shaken violently. The earth reels to and fro like a drunkard and it totters like a shack, for its transgression is heavy upon it, and it will fall, never to rise again (Isaiah 24:17-20).

Jeremiah wrote:

> "Terror, pit and snare are coming upon you, O inhabitant of Moab," declares the LORD. "The one who flees from the terror will fall into the pit, and the one who climbs up out of the pit will be caught in the snare; for I shall bring upon her, even upon Moab, the year of their punishment," declares the LORD (Jeremiah 48:43-44)

Now, look at this. I find it to be most remarkable...

We just reviewed a thorough denunciation and report of God's plan to destroy Moab. He was going to humiliate them, wreck their economy, send them into exile, destroy their idolatry and apparently end them as a nation. But look! At the end of this oracle, God, in a few words, without details, promised restoration.

> "Yet I will restore the fortunes of Moab in the latter days," declares the LORD (Jeremiah 48:47a).

What was God's attitude? Even in His wrath the LORD was heartbroken over the coming destruction of an idolatrous, arrogant, cruel enemy of His uniquely covenanted people. He promised to utterly destroy and disperse Moab. But wait! He promised to restore their fortunes in the latter days. The Hebrew speaks of God ending Moab's exile and restoring them.[10] It is the same word, used within the same context, found earlier in Jeremiah[11] and in the seminal oracle of Deuteronomy 30.

> "I will be found by you," declares the LORD, "and I will restore your fortunes and will gather you from all the nations and from all the places where I have driven you," declares the LORD, "and I will bring you back to the place from where I sent you into exile" (Jeremiah 29:14).

> ... the LORD your God will restore you from captivity, and have compassion on you, and will gather you again from all the peoples where the LORD your God has scattered you (Deuteronomy 30:3).

What a pattern!

What Jeremiah foretold concerning Moab closely followed the prophetic prototype pertaining to Israel. Not only Moab, but the same wording is used to describe God's redemptive dealings with Ammon, Elam, Egypt, Samaria and... Sodom![12]

Why mention this?

Through this example we can see that God's dealings with the nations are first exemplified in His relationship to the Jewish people. This is true in the denunciation of pride, idolatry, cruelty and in the unequivocal judgment manifest in destruction and diaspora. As with the Jewish people, the

> *As with the Jewish people, the outcome of His dealings with the nations (exemplified in Moab) is restoration.*

outcome of His dealings with the nations (exemplified in Moab) is restoration.

It is apparent that there is only one nation that must be blessed or judged according to specific covenant stipulations.

> You only have I known of all the families of the earth; therefore, I will punish you for all your iniquities (Amos 3:2, ESV).

However, God loves and will ultimately "know" all nations as nations, not just as individuals gathered from the nations. One reason He chose Abraham was so the families of the earth would be blessed. It is also certain that God will ultimately judge the nations[13] as well as each individual.[14] God may judge them in this intermediate time, before the final judgments, too. As Paul wrote concerning individuals:

> There will be tribulation and distress for every soul of man who does evil, of the Jew first and also of the Greek, but glory and honor and peace to everyone who does good, to the Jew first and also to the Greek. For there is no partiality with God (Romans 2:9-11).

Moab is only one example of God's revealed interaction with other nations besides Israel. When explored, we see that there is a revelation of a relationship with the world that is established through, and patterned after, His relationship with the Jewish people.

So...is it, "Yes," or, "No"?

The people of Israel provide the pattern of being loved, chastised or judged and restored to a place of glory beyond their imaginations.[15] If it's true for Israel, then to some degree it is true for the nations. For instance, God testified that He brought other nations from one place to another and enabled them to conquer and settle land.

> "Are you not as the sons of Ethiopia to Me, O sons of Israel?" declares the LORD. "Have I not brought up Israel from the land of Egypt, and the Philistines from Caphtor and the Arameans from Kir?" (Amos 9:7)

Obviously, the Philistines and Arameans were not brought out and settled with the same majestic acts of power as Israel was from Egypt.

> And what one nation on the earth is like Your people Israel, whom God went to redeem for Himself as a people and to make a name for Himself, and to do a great thing for You and awesome things for Your land, before Your people whom You have redeemed for Yourself from Egypt, from nations and their gods? For You have established for Yourself Your people Israel as Your own people forever, and You, O LORD, have become their God (2 Samuel 7:23-24).

Nevertheless, a pattern was established in the Exodus.

We can see God's hand at work in divinely determined national boundaries.

> ...He made from one man every nation of mankind to live on all the face of the earth, having determined their appointed times and the boundaries of their habitation (Acts 17:26).

Israel: A Servant People

Prophetic and priestly people exemplify and experience God's interactions on behalf of others. This is the case with Israel. All Scripture pertaining to the Jewish people can be applied with good conscience to any person or group that either knows the Lord or has apostatized. Israel's histories and oracles should be highly prized as a primary means of edification. They are valuable. Analogies can be applied to individuals, families, churches (and perhaps nations) in a God honoring way that does not distort or distract from the text's intention. However, the actual message should not be devalued.

Again, there is nothing wrong with applying verses concerning God's love for the Jewish people, or "Zion" or "Jerusalem" to one's own situation. However, the Church often finds the allegories and parables arising from those sections of Scripture to be more exciting than the writings themselves. For instance, which is more encouraging to the average believer, that they should "rise and shine for their light has come," or that this oracle describes Israel's destiny?

> Arise, shine; for your light has come, and the glory of the LORD has risen upon you. For behold, darkness will cover the earth and deep darkness the peoples; but the LORD will rise upon you and His glory will appear upon you. Nations will come to your light, and kings to the brightness of your rising (Isaiah 60:1-3).

How many times have you heard Isaiah 60:1-3 applied to individuals, churches, movements or denominations? Compare that to the number of times you have heard this enthusiastically preached or prophesied concerning the Jewish people? What was Isaiah actually prophesying?

God is watching over the corporate heart of His transnational people. Paul instructed the Gentile believers about Israel's destiny and the effects it would have on the rest of the world. By doing this, God sought to ensure that the entire church would highly value and long for Israel's salvation. Paul wrote:

God sought to ensure that the entire Church would highly value and long for Israel's salvation.

> Now if their transgression is riches for the world and their failure is riches for the Gentiles, how much more will their fulfillment be! But I am speaking to you who are Gentiles. Inasmuch then as I am an apostle of Gentiles, I magnify my ministry, if somehow I might

> move to jealousy my fellow countrymen and save some of them. For if their rejection is the reconciliation of the world, what will their acceptance be but life from the dead? (Romans 11:12-15)

As the Church comes into agreement with Paul's unpacking of the Hebrew prophets, they will hunger and thirst for Israel's salvation. Not just because of their identification and fellowship with God's heart. Not because of idealistic altruism. No, they will hunger and thirst for Israel's national redemption because Paul convinced them of the blessing that will transpire when these oracles are fulfilled. Romans emphatically reveals that the road leading to the release of "greater riches for the world" (11:12), and "life from the dead" (11:15), is only entered through the narrow gate of Israel's national reconciliation to the Messiah.

If God is not content to begin the future age of greater blessing until Israel comes "in", we can also see that He isn't going to leave any nation "out."

> A partial hardening has happened to Israel until the fullness of the Gentiles has come in; and so all Israel will be saved (Romans 11:25b-26a).

God wants all nations to experience the greater riches He has in store. God wants the whole cosmos to experience "life from the dead." He is calling for international reconciliation to begin in the Church through Gentile believers' enthused commitment to Israel's salvation and wellbeing. To reiterate: the blessed destiny of the nations and the resurrection glory of God being manifest in the earth is tied to the Jewish people's spiritual restoration. God will

The blessed destiny of the nations and the resurrection glory of God being manifest in the earth is tied to the Jewish people's spiritual restoration. God will not be content until this happens and neither should the Church.

not be content until this happens and neither should the Church.

God's Overall Objective: Glory

When God pardoned Israel through Moses' intercession, He divulged that He intended His glory to fill the earth. He said:

> But indeed, as I live, all the earth will be filled with the glory of the LORD (Numbers 14:21).

The psalmist connected the manifestation of glory throughout the earth to the God of Israel working wonders on behalf of His people.

> Blessed be the LORD God, the God of Israel, Who alone works wonders. And blessed be His glorious name forever; and may the whole earth be filled with His glory. Amen, and Amen (Psalm 72:18-19).

Ultimately, after the Redeemer comes, removes ungodliness from Jacob, and Israel is transgenerationally restored (Isaiah 59:20-21), progressively increasing glory shall be released amongst the pilgrim nations.

> Arise, shine; for your light has come, and the glory of the LORD has risen upon you. For behold, darkness will cover the earth and deep darkness the peoples; but the LORD will rise upon you And His glory will appear upon you. Nations will come to your light, and kings to the brightness of your rising (Isaiah 60:1-3).

Ezekiel rehearsed this prophetic pattern: When glory returns to Israel, the earth shines "with His glory."

> Then he led me to the gate, the gate facing toward the east; and behold, the glory of the God of Israel was coming from the way of the east. And His voice was like the sound of many waters; and the earth shone with His glory (Ezekiel 43:1-2).

Prophesying God's judgments and redemption, Habakkuk gave the outcome of God's work:

> For the Earth will be filled with the knowledge of the glory of the LORD, As the waters cover the sea (Habakkuk 2:14).

God's evident desire for relationship with Israel is representative of God's desire for relationship with every people group. This is how the Great Commission is to be understood: God loves the nations. The commencing of the new age (greater riches, life from the dead) does not begin until "the fullness of the Gentiles comes in (Romans 11:25b)" due to the fulfillment of the Great Commission (Matthew 24:14; 28:18-20).

Israel's corporate salvation will not happen until the fullness of the Gentiles come in. The saving of the remnant (fullness?) of all nations is important for the sake of Israel, just as Israel's restoration is important for the sake of the cosmos.

Every individual who is in relationship to Jesus is connected to Israel's destiny. God includes each of them in the blessed aftermath of this age's consummation and the commencement of the next. His triumphant war on behalf of Israel ushers in a much fuller manifestation of the Kingdom in which all Gentile believers will participate, because God shall fulfill His confirmed promises to the patriarchs and their progeny.

> For I say that the Messiah has become a servant to the circumcision on behalf of the truth of God to confirm the promises given to the fathers, and for the Gentiles to glorify God for His mercy;
>
> as it is written, "THEREFORE I WILL GIVE PRAISE TO YOU AMONG THE GENTILES, AND I WILL SING TO YOUR NAME."
>
> Again, he says, "REJOICE, O GENTILES, WITH HIS PEOPLE."

> And again, "PRAISE THE LORD ALL YOU GENTILES, AND LET ALL THE PEOPLES PRAISE HIM."
>
> Again, Isaiah says, "THERE SHALL COME THE ROOT OF JESSE, AND HE WHO ARISES TO RULE OVER THE GENTILES, IN HIM SHALL THE GENTILES HOPE" (Romans 15:8-12).

Meanwhile, God reveals His love for the Jewish people to the Gentile Church. The degree of their love for God will determine how the revelation of His love for Israel affects them. As the final days approach, God is revealing His love for the Jewish people to the Gentile Church. Paul was the Apostle to the Gentiles. As their apostle, he made certain they knew that the Scriptures pertaining to Israel remained relevant.

How did Paul do this? To answer, let's first look at the Messiah's affirmation of Wisdom Literature. Then we'll see that Paul's validation of the prophetic Scriptures followed a similar pattern.

Jesus brought the principles of Wisdom Literature into the life of His followers. He said, "Give and it will be given to you" (Luke 6:38a). In that statement, the Messiah endorsed the scriptural principles pertaining to sowing and reaping.

Paul joined Jesus' affirmation of Israel's sages when he wrote:

> The one who is taught the word is to share all good things with the one who teaches him. Do not be deceived, God is not mocked; for whatever a man sows, this he will also reap. For the one who sows to his own flesh will from the flesh reap corruption, but the one who sows to the Spirit will from the Spirit reap eternal life. Let us not lose heart in doing good, for in due time we will reap if we do not grow weary (Galatians 6:6-9).

Through the Messiah's endorsement and an apostle's affirmation, the whole of Wisdom Literature was dignified and made relevant to Jesus' disciples.

Something similar has happened through what has seemed to be mere throwaway lines in Romans. There is more power than most realize in this radical statement:

> From the standpoint of the gospel they are enemies for your sake, but from the standpoint of God's choice they are beloved for the sake of the fathers; for the gifts and the calling of God are irrevocable (Romans 11:28-29).

Paul wrote that Jewish people who have yet to follow Jesus are beloved for the sake of the patriarchs. What did that surprising, inspired, authoritative evaluation do? It made every Scripture about the love God has for Israel (each passage and every prophecy predicated upon that love's reality) relevant to the church's view of the Jewish people throughout the ages.

Does God love other nations for the sake of godly ancestors? Perhaps, but it is not mentioned in the New Testament. Since it is not specifically taught, it would be reckless to declare that we know it to be the case. As far as we can ascertain, this type of love is exclusive to Israel.

Paul did affirm God's sovereign mercy and provision for all nations (Acts 17:24-31). However, nothing in the New Testament is comparable to Romans 11:28-29 ("loved for the sake of the patriarchs"). So, at the very least, this is a unique form of love, reinforced in Romans, which is different from the love that motivates individual redemption. This is a "national" love (Deuteronomy 7:7-8) that, when requited, shall bring about "life from the dead" (Romans 11:15).

In geopolitical prophecy both prophets and angels testify that the Lord shall return to the Mount of Olives. Apparently, there are, as of yet, unfulfilled prophecies about a war waged against Israel that will provoke the coming of the Lord. By way of comparison, with all due respect, God loves Belgium, but the

In geopolitical prophecy both prophets and angels testify that the Lord shall return to the Mount of Olives.

world could be marshaled against Belgium and Jesus will not physically return to rescue them. However, it is written that this is what shall transpire in a final battle of the nations against Jerusalem.[16]

While this is so, so also is this: Israel is related in filial fashion to every nation on the planet. Israel is God's firstborn nation, not God's only child.

Jacob uniquely loved Joseph. He especially loved Benjamin, as well. He loved Judah and his other children, too. In fact, the Patriarch prophesied that the Messiah would come through Judah, not Joseph. Just because Joseph was singled out as the firstborn[17] did not mean that Jacob was apathetic about the wellbeing of the rest of his children.

However, when Joseph's older brothers could no longer stand the favor uniquely shown him, they threw Joseph in a pit, sold him into slavery and acted throughout much of their adult life as if Joseph was dead. They made up a lie and acted like they believed it. This fiction continued until they could no longer deny that Joseph was alive and had to confess that one of the foundations of the way they lived their lives was based on a falsehood. I appeal to the Gentile Church, wake up! Israel lives and the Father is awaiting the restoration of these who are uniquely loved for the sake of the Patriarchs.

Consider This:

Children carry the same DNA as their father. Within every child of God is a love for all nations and a unique love for the Jewish people. There are many ways to express this love.

Perhaps there may be a root of resentment in you concerning God's unique love for His people. Remember, while this unique love exists, it is the pattern of God's love for *all* nations. If you find this resentment in your heart, repent and by faith receive the living God's love for Israel. He is looking for those with whom He may fellowship concerning this matter of His heart. And it is a serious matter to misrepresent the heart of God, as we shall see in the next chapter.

5

Misrepresenting God's Heart

IN 1992, I READ THIS:

> Adolph Hitler died a Roman Catholic and an annual mass is celebrated in his memory in Madrid. Hermann Goering died a Lutheran.[18]

Surprised? I was, and a bit saddened, a bit upset, a bit incredulous. Here is another question: Were the following two statements really written by the same person?

> When we are inclined to boast of our position [as Christians] we should remember that we are but Gentiles, while the Jews are of the lineage of Christ. We are aliens and in-laws; they are blood relatives, cousins, and brothers of our Lord. Therefore, if one is to boast of flesh and blood the Jews are actually nearer to Christ than we are.[19]

> What shall we Christians do with this rejected and condemned people, the Jews? I shall give you my sincere advice: First, their synagogue or school is to be set on fire and what won't burn is to be heaped over with dirt and dumped on, so that no one can see a stone or chunk of it forever...in honor of our Lord and of Christendom, so that God might see that we are Christians...[20]

The author of both statements was Martin Luther. Luther was, paradoxically, one of the most noted heroes and, perhaps, the most malevolent theologian in the history of Protestantism.[21] He began as a lover of the Jewish people and became the primary anti-Semite of his age. His hatred of the Jewish people reflected and influenced Germany's culture and his words were part of the Nazi party's apologetic. His malice is felt to this day. I was taught that Luther was an anomaly. When I was younger, I expected his despicable example would keep the true Christian from the same deplorable mistakes. Not so.

Born again...Nazis?

As a young man, I wanted to understand the language of the New Testament. This big box was delivered, and I unpacked the ten volumes of the Theological Dictionary of the New Testament (TDNT) called, "Kittel's." What an unexpected trove of scholarship. There was more information than I could use in one lifetime. Who were these people who knew so much? I found out that Dr. Kittel, the editor of the initial volumes of TDNT, for whom the dictionary is popularly named, was a Nazi. I was astonished.

This Nazi was raised as a pietist and believed orthodox Lutheran doctrine.[22] Kittel was not only a believer, he was also a New Testament scholar. Not only was he a New Testament scholar (one of the most respected of his generation), but he was the scion of a renowned Old Testament scholar. Not only was he a New Testament scholar, the son of an Old Testament scholar, but Kittel was an expert in rabbinic literature. And this believer, a son of an Old Testament scholar, a prestigious New Testament scholar and expert in rabbinic literature was a Nazi.

Here is some more information about Kittel:

> From the beginning, he devoted himself to the study of the Jewish roots of early Christianity...He called for collaboration between Jewish scholars of rabbinic tradition and scholars of early Christianity. Kittel wrote a book that was "dedicated to the memory of the rabbi

> and scholar Israel I. Kahan, with whom Kittel had had a long working relationship."[23]

In *Problems of Late Palestinian Judaism and Early Christianity*, published in 1926, dedicated to Rabbi Kahan, Kittel stated, "Jesus is a Palestinian Jew...he and his disciples belonged to Palestinian Judaism..."[24] Yet he wrote,

> Jesus has deep roots in the Israelite Jewish background, but the fulfillment of his self-consciousness means the end of his ethnic and religious Judaism.[25]

That is an amazing statement. Dr. Kittel wrote that as soon as Jesus knew who He really was, He ceased to be a Jew.

I find Kittel's conclusion to be incredible. Let's interact with this by reading John 20:16-17 from Kittel's perspective. First, the Bible reads:

> Jesus said to her, "Mary."
>
> She turned and said to him in Aramaic, "Rabboni!" (which means Teacher).
>
> Jesus said to her, "Do not cling to me, for I have not yet ascended to the Father; but go to my brothers and say to them, 'I am ascending to my Father and your Father, to my God and your God.'"

Perhaps, from Kittel's perspective, this narrative might have been reported like this:

> *Jesus said to her, "Mary."*
>
> *She turned and said to him in Aramaic, "Rabboni!" (which means Teacher).*
>
> *Jesus replied in Latin, "Why call me, 'Rabbi'? I'm not Jewish! I left those ethnic and religious grave clothes in the tomb!"*

Surely, if there was a moment God incarnate would have shed an immature developing self-consciousness and ended "his ethnic and religious Judaism" it would have been after His resurrection. Instead, what do we find when we read John's report? A Rabbi. This resurrected Messiah did not correct how Mary addressed Him. Jesus was a resurrected rabbi.

Returning to Kittel, in 1933, seven years after he wrote *Problems of Late Palestinian Judaism and Early Christianity*, he officially joined the Nazi party. He enthusiastically endorsed the Nazi program "for removing Jews from all parts of Germany's professional, governmental, and educational life."[26]

Learning from History

Surely Dr. Kittel's appalling example prevents Christian theologians from making the same mistake. Alas, one cannot help but see a correlation between Kittel and the current advocacy of boycotting, divesting and sanctioning Israel by some leading New Testament scholars.

One cannot help but see a correlation between Kittel and the current advocacy of boycotting, divesting and sanctioning Israel by some leading New Testament scholars.

There was an ancient Christian legend that Nero would be resurrected and become the antichrist. The legend was named, "Nero Redivivus." This current phenomenon is like "Kittel Redivivus." This time, the motivation is not racialist. Instead, it seems to be sparked by politically liberal Christians. They apparently find common cause with Islam against what they believe to be an anachronistic leftover of Western imperialism: the state of Israel.

When one listens to the current group of 21st century anti-

Israel scholars they convey the appearance of passion for "justice." However, their tone and message communicate a theological and geo-political arrogance towards the Jewish people and the state of Israel. They are not crying out for the extermination of the Jews. Well, neither did Kittel, the enabler of the Nazi agenda. He was a Nazi, just not quite as extreme... at least in the beginning.

At one point Nazi Kittel thought he was trying to do the Jewish people a service by promoting a form of segregation. This would promote a "racial purity" of the Jewish people. Today, Christian antagonists of Israel say they are not against Jews or Judaism, just the Zionist State. They demonize Israel, making awkward analogies to Nazi Germany. They claim they do not intend to harm Jews. They say they are doing Israelis a favor by encouraging nations to boycott, divest from and sanction Israel. All the while, they offer comfort and encouragement to those with evident genocidal intent. In their view, only the unsophisticated think it looks like hatred. Some of their best friends are Jews who agree with them.

Kittel did not consider himself a villain. And it is necessary to recall that he was brilliant. Yet he came to this:

> Kittel the Party member urges the removal of all Jews from academic and professional life. Recognizing that this "solution" to the "Jewish question" would result in great suffering—but never publicly acknowledging the existence of the extermination camps—he urges kindness toward individuals, and indeed acts himself to help a few Jewish persons to escape...[27]

Consider... Kittel rescued individual Jews. Kittel upheld the ideology, party and policies dedicated to their slaughter. He lived this contradiction from a highly nuanced, well-informed, classical Christian theology.

Despite his being a Nazi, the *Theological Dictionary of the*

New Testament is not a racially anti-Semitic work. However, I do find it bizarre that in its first volume the entry on "agape" (love) was written by Stauffer "who was active in the German Christian movement".[28] This movement was a "big tent" which had one common denominator: they were Nazis. Do you find it ironic that multitudes get their definition of "agape" from a Nazi? Really, I do not know whether to laugh or cry. One friend said, "Laugh and cry." Join us.

To this day Nazi Kittel's name is associated with a monumental piece of scholarship. His name is honored although his Fuhrer's is excoriated. Whole denominations derive their name from the notorious anti-Semite, Martin Luther.

Answer me. Would someone name a theological dictionary after an infamous pedophile? Would we name a religious movement for a felon who ran a Ponzi-scheme? Sadly, being an Anti-Semite is not that abhorrent to the Church. If these matters never bothered you it may indicate that either a) you did not have this information, or b) you are accustomed to Christian Anti-Semitism.

Sadly, being an Anti-Semite is not that abhorrent to the Church.

An Anomaly

I became a disciple of Jesus in a Jewish-friendly environment. I was told one could not be a Christian and hate anyone, much less hate the Jewish people. I was told, "true Christians love the Jewish people." I fear that I am the bearer of bad news: being a believer in Jesus, knowing the Old Testament and the social and cultural background of the New Testament, studying in the best schools, being an expert on the text and being a member of a believing church does not disqualify one from being a hater of the

Jewish people.

In the 1500's Luther's anti-Semitism was not perceived as strange. In mid-20th century Germany Kittel's conclusions aroused no outrage. Their theological heirs are respected. People are still "Lutherans." Students, scholars and clergy study "Kittel's." Seen within the context of 1,900 years, the anomaly is that there is a believing Christian, trans-denominational movement that is philo-Semitic, not one that is anti-Semitic. We have been living in the midst of a historical abnormality for a long time. Who knows how long this love of the Jewish people will last?

In the beginning of the Second World War, Nazi Kittel and others interpreted German victories as evidence that God was blessing Hitler and the Reich. In parallel, one revered New Testament scholar recently wryly said before an assembly of scholars,

> You walk into the Jewish quarter in West Jerusalem today, and start talking about the way Israel's God is now acting through Lebanon, Syria, Jordan, and Egypt and I suspect you'll get a pretty dusty response.

This was intended to be ironic. It elicited laughter. Here is my interpretation of this "wise"-crack:

> *The God of Israel is acting through the nation of Israel's enemies. God is actually against the Jewish state. The joke is on them.*

As you may suppose, I do not find this amusing. That a venerated Christian leader should mock Israel's supposed misunderstanding of God's intentions in this era of threatened eradication and genocidal intent is unworthy of the Messiah. Isn't it? I do not believe his statement is right, but if what the theologian said was true, shouldn't it provoke intercession and not snickering? Please do not get angry. Rather, mourn with me over the spiritual state of these evangelical smart people. By the way, how do you think God felt? Ask Him.

What is God's intent in this hour? Is He directly involved in the reestablishing of the nation of Israel? Should we believe that the Ruler of the Nations is motivating the Muslim nations, and much of the rest of the world, to hate Israel? Is He the author of this animosity? Perhaps there is some oracle of which I am unaware that foretells,

> *Finally, O Israel, I will cause you to mimic biblical prophecy, to deceive Bible-believing Christians, but My purpose is to destroy you.*

Or, dare we hope that this is the time to favor Zion? Is it time to comfort His people? Is this the beginning of a restoration of the Jewish people to the Land and then to the Messiah? There are Scriptural end-time prophecies of international outrage over a Jewish Jerusalem. In those prophecies, you cannot find a hint that the God of the Patriarchs is raising up this anti-Israel inter-national alliance to chastise the Jewish people. There is no correspondence between the way Babylon was a tool in God's hand and the prophesied end-time alignments of antagonistic nations. What we find in the Bible is a strand of prophecy that speaks of the God of Israel gathering the nations together against Israel. Here is part of some overlooked origins of that prophetic theme:

You cannot find a hint that the God of the Patriarchs is raising up this anti-Israel international alliance to chastise the Jewish people.

> The LORD of hosts has sworn saying, "Surely, just as I have intended so it has happened, and just as I have planned so it will stand, to break Assyria in My land, and I will trample him on My mountains. Then his yoke will be removed from them and his

> burden removed from their shoulder.
>
> This is the plan devised against the whole earth; and this is the hand that is stretched out against all the nations. For the LORD of hosts has planned, and who can frustrate it? And as for His stretched-out hand, who can turn it back?" (Isaiah 14:4-27).

Commentators on this passage tend to emphasize verse 27: "For the LORD of hosts has planned, and who can frustrate it? And as for His stretched-out hand, who can turn it back?" This verse is stressed because it depicts "the sovereignty of God." However, they rarely remark on the earlier verses, especially, "This is the plan devised against the whole earth; and this is the hand that is stretched out against all the nations." I wonder, "Why?"

This passage prophesies two things

1. The destruction of Assyria on the mountains of Judah.
2. That the method and the location of Assyria's destruction is the pattern for all the nations of the earth.

One does not have to arduously search the Prophets to find this out: If God is gathering all the nations of the earth against Jerusalem, it may very well be that it is to destroy their power, not to "chastise" Israel.[29]

Be Circumspect

In Jeremiah, we find a presumptuous people misplacing their confidence in "the Temple of the LORD." They believed Jerusalem would never fall because God's house was there. The prophet warned:

> Do not trust in deceptive words, saying,

> "This is the temple of the LORD,
> the temple of the LORD,
> the temple of the LORD." (Jeremiah 7:4)

Those convinced the details of the divine plan are easily discerned are deceived. When the Jewish people assumed God would protect them from Babylon, or Rome, they were tragically mistaken. They refused to believe Jeremiah's and Jesus' judgment oracles. In the light of this history, many well-meaning Christians are persuaded that much of the Church has embraced a ridiculous enthusiasm and a false hope.

Yet, those who see this as a repetition of millenarian deception may inadvertently mirror the same error. Perhaps they are those guilty of false confidence. They presume God is finished with Israel. They presume that current affairs are a series of unfortunate events, coincidences, misleading the gullible to erroneous conclusions. They presume that those who believe God will ultimately defend Israel have refused to learn from history. They presume that those who believe God is doing a restorative work are analogous to the inhabitants of Jerusalem in the time of Nebuchadnezzar, or Titus. Perhaps they are the ones who are wrong.

It is possible to know the Scriptures and believe the gospel, and still misread God's intent. If God is in the process of restoring the Jewish people then the one misinterpreting the text is the supersessionist. If God is in the process of restoring Israel, then the spirit motivating the hatred of Israel is not from above. However, the God revealed in the Bible can use the wrath of fallen angels and the pride of powerful nations to bring about prophetic preconditions for the physical manifestation of His Kingdom.

> His hand is stretched out against all the nations,
> He has devised a plan against the whole earth (Isaiah 14:26).

Where is wisdom? I believe that wisdom discerns this: principalities of Christian anti-Semitism are at work today. Historically, most of the Church has been defiled through communion with these spiritual malevolencies. I believe that wisdom informs us that Father God is looking for friends with whom He can share His heart concerning the Jewish people. Will you be one of them? Will you allow the Lord to remove blind spots regarding the clear truths written in the New Testament? Yes, I believe you will!

> *Father God is looking for friends with whom He can share His heart concerning the Jewish people. Will you be one of them?*

6

The Seven Blessings

ROMANS 9:4-5 SUMS UP GOD'S DEVOTED INTERACTION with the Jewish people. They present a window to His heart, a key to Israel's future, and offer insight into the value He places upon His people. To the Church over the centuries this has been a blind spot, but in recent years the Lord is revealing His heart.

Macular Degeneration

I am going to briefly contrast what Paul wrote with the primary position traditionally held by the Church after New Testament times. Supersessionism (Replacement Theology) is the conventional view of the historic churches. This point of view influences the vision of multitudes. Since the Holocaust whole denominations have modified their vision. However, the same emotional and cultural needs that motivated supersessionism are very much alive. These successfully block the light that streams from the Scriptures. Supersessionism prevents the believer from fellowship with God's heart concerning the Jewish people.

Depending upon how significant this blind spot is to the God of Abraham, Isaac, and Israel, it could be a substantial spiritual problem. Macular degeneration results in blindness in the center of the field of vision. This disease does not make a person totally sightless. However, it prevents those so afflicted from recognizing faces and interpreting the expressions of those faces. I believe the same thing has happened with those who misunderstand fundamental aspects of God's heart for the Jewish people. We need to maintain and cultivate affection for brethren who are blinded to this aspect of God's heart. Concerning blindness, not only are believers forbidden to mislead a blind person, we are also enjoined to never put a stumbling block in front of someone who is visually impaired.[30] Let us recognize that everybody has blind spots. We only see an allotted measure of spiritual reality.[31] Friends can gently point out blind spots to each other.

We believe that Paul's vison was clearer than ours. What did he see concerning the Jewish people? Look at Romans 9:4-5:

> [They] are Israelites, to whom belongs the adoption as sons, and the glory and the covenants and the giving of the Law and the temple service and the promises, whose are the fathers, and from whom is the Christ according to the flesh, who is over all, God blessed forever. Amen.

"The Seven"

In these two verses, we see seven attributes of one people. It is generally believed that, biblically, the number "7" represents completion. Let us count them. These people (Israel) are characterized by: 1) a relationship (adoption); 2) the exuberant radiance of God's goodness (glory); 3) a ratifying of that relationship (covenants); 4) a regulating of that relationship (Torah); 5) rituals that maintained and expressed that relationship (worship); 6) the destiny resulting from that relationship (promises); 7) the roots of that relationship (patriarchs).

Let us call them, "The Seven." Following "The Seven," Paul pointed out an amazing outcome of this relationship: The Savior of the world, the Messiah of Israel, God becoming incarnate. Paul made certain that the recipients of this letter would know that the coming of Jesus did not render "The Seven" obsolete. They "are" (present tense) Israelites. To them "belongs" (present tense) this list describing their "gifts and calling" even after the Messiah's advent.

Many call these unique identity markers, "privileges." Here are two examples:

> Paul begins by reasserting his personal concern for his people and reminding his readers of Israel's own covenant privileges in which they were now participants—that is, in Israel's covenant privileges.[32]

> ... the incongruity between the Jews' present status and their marvelous privileges.[33]

"The Seven" are the results of God's affection and jealous desire for Israel. They are blessings lavished upon His beloved. They are gifts, motivated by love, given for the purpose of securing, developing and maintaining a loving relationship with Himself. Each of "The Seven" were bestowed in a manner analogous to God's tender heart expressed in Ezekiel:

> "I also clothed you with embroidered cloth and put sandals of porpoise skin on your feet; and I wrapped you with fine linen and covered you with silk. I adorned you with ornaments, put bracelets on your hands and a necklace around your neck. I also put a ring in your nostril, earrings in your ears and a beautiful crown on your head. Thus

> you were adorned with gold and silver, and your dress was of fine linen, silk and embroidered cloth. You ate fine flour, honey and oil; so you were exceedingly beautiful and advanced to royalty. Then your fame went forth among the nations on account of your beauty, for it was perfect because of My splendor which I bestowed on you," declares the Lord GOD (Ezekiel 16:10-14).

"The Seven" were unearned expressions of God's devoted attraction to Israel. They were imparted because the LORD loves them.

"Loves," or "Loved?"

Please note the tense. Paul first writes, "who are Israelites." Then he uses a word which is translated "whose are," or, "to whom belong." Both the context and the tense of the Greek do not allow for an interpretation that puts "The Seven" in the past. Paul taught that these blessings belong to Israel. No archaeologist has found an early copy of Romans which differs from what has been preserved here. The present tense, "belongs," must be maintained to understand the apostle's intent.

Both the context and the tense of the Greek do not allow for an interpretation that puts "The Seven" in the past. Paul taught that these blessings belong to Israel.

See how the past tense reads differently than what was written. Interacting with Paul's words, those who embrace Replacement Theology must rewrite those verses, perhaps thusly:

> *They used to be Israelites.*
>
> *The Church is the newly reconstituted Israel of God. We are the true Israelites, and the adoption as sons belongs to the Church.*
>
> *Let Paul write instead, "Whose was the glory," for the glory belongs to the Church. The covenants used to belong to them, but now the only covenant that has any relevance to us belongs to the Church.*
>
> *Although the Law was theirs, now the Scriptures rightfully belong to the Church.*
>
> *Let it be written, "Whose was the temple worship," for we are the spiritual reality of which the temple was a shadow. Temple worship is totally irrelevant.*[34]
>
> *At one time the promises pertained to the Jews, but now every promised blessing belongs to the Church. The patriarchs were theirs, now we are the true children of Abraham, Isaac and Jacob. Jesus Christ came through the Jewish people. We honor and thank our gracious heavenly Father for accomplishing this through such unworthy people.*

Supersessionism's stance is adversarial to Paul's position. Replacement Theology relegates "The Seven" to the Jewish people's past and applies "The Seven" to the church's present and future. Paul deliberately emphasized the present tense and claimed them for the Jewish people. Please read it again.

> [They] are Israelites, to whom belongs the adoption as sons,

> and the glory
>
> and the covenants
>
> and the giving of the Law
>
> and the temple service
>
> and the promises,
>
> whose are the fathers,
>
> and from whom is the Christ according to the flesh, who is over all, God blessed forever. Amen (Romans 9:4-5).

The Overlooked, Exceptional Blessing

Everything Paul listed led to the summum bonum of this list. Unlike "The Seven" it is not the blessing of possessing. Rather, Paul focuses our vision on how the world was blessed through Israel. This is the exceptional blessing: the Jewish people were chosen to bring the Messiah into the world. The apostle focuses our attention on the outstanding honor God has given. This is Israel's supreme shining glory. It is the most precious of all Paul mentioned. Compared to this, "The Seven" fade into an obscure, peripheral position.

> ...and from whom is the Christ according to the flesh, who is over all, God blessed forever. Amen (Romans 9:5b).

Do you recall the Magnifat? The song of Jesus' mother has been rehearsed and meditated upon for practically 2,000 years. Here is the start of her worship as translated in the Complete Jewish Bible:

> Then Miryam said,
> "My soul magnifies ADONAI;
> and my spirit rejoices in God, my Savior,
> who has taken notice of his servant-girl
> in her humble position.
> For- imagine it! – from now on,
> all generations will call me blessed!
> (Luke 1:46-48)

Although the Greek might not *strictly* allow, "imagine it," an appropriate sense of wonder is captured in this rendering.

> For—imagine it!—from now on,
> all generations will call me blessed!
> (Luke 1:48b)

Mary was a faith-filled Jewish adolescent who, in her innocent devotion, represented the faithful remnant of Israel. She saw her role in redemption's history as uniquely blessed. Multitudes over ensuing centuries have used this canticle as a foundation of their devotional life. It is ironic that the same "masses" blithely skip through what Paul was saying here. To understand the honor Paul said belonged to Israel, please imagine along with me... Tell me, what if Romans 9:5b was written differently? Let's experiment and change it to this:

> *...and from the Virgin Mary is the Christ according to the flesh, who is over all, God blessed forever. Amen (Romans 9:5b).*

If Paul wrote that, it would have been one of the most famous verses in the Bible. It would have been memorized, catechized, sung, prayed, taught and been the foundation of encyclicals. However, this fragment, "and from whom is the Christ according to the flesh," is the source of a collective yawn. It is not a source of meditation; it is taken for granted and considered irrelevant. It shouldn't be. This verse is a revelation of God's love for Israel.

And what an honor. I'm hard-pressed to imagine a greater privilege than to be chosen to bring the Messiah into the world. God arranged sacred history that Jesus would be for Israel's glory. Look at this prophetic description of Jesus:

> "...a light, for revelation to the Gentiles, and for glory to your people Israel" (Luke 2:32, NET).

The glory of Israel is the light of revelation to the nations. The glory proceeding from Israel enlightens the nations. The glory of Israel is Jesus. The honor of being the people who brought the Messiah into the world is worthy of appreciation and celebration. Romans 9:5b should be a source of meditation. In it the heart of God is revealed. It is as if Father said,

The honor of being the people who brought the Messiah into the world is worthy of appreciation and celebration.

> *What shall I do for Abraham, My friend?*
>
> *I shall bestow honor on his offspring. The world will know of My love for them and My love for their descendants.*
>
> *My Son shall become flesh through them. He shall be part of this family. He is the son of David, the son of Jesse...the son of Judah, the son of Jacob, the son of Isaac, the son of Abraham My friend.*

In our culture, this may make little sense. In the history of Israel such a thing is not unheard of. Look at this narrative from 2 Samuel:

> The king said, "Is there not yet anyone of the house of Saul to whom I may show the kindness of God?" And Ziba said to the king, "There is still a son of Jonathan who is crippled in both feet."
>
> So the king said to him, "Where is he?" And Ziba said to the king, "Behold, he is in the house of Machir the son of Ammiel in Lo-debar."
>
> Then King David sent and brought him from the house of Machir the son of Ammiel, from Lo-debar. Mephibosheth, the son of Jonathan the son of Saul, came to David and fell on his face and prostrated himself.
>
> And David said, "Mephibosheth." And he said, "Here is your servant!" David said to him, "Do not fear, for I will surely show kindness to you for the sake of your father Jonathan, and will restore to you all the land of your grandfather Saul; and you shall eat at my table regularly" (2 Samuel 9:3-7).

Here is an example of bestowing honor upon a descendent of a covenant partner. Jonathan's son was honored for Jonathan's sake. David's loyalty and honor reflected the God who honors Israel for the sake of the Patriarchs. God's heart towards the Patriarchs is more like David's towards Jonathan than how He is misrepresented

Jonathan's son was honored for Jonathan's sake. David's loyalty and honor reflected the God who honors Israel for the sake of the Patriarchs.

by those who, in contrast to Paul, answer this in the affirmative:

> I say then, God has not rejected His people, has He? May it never be! (Romans 11:1a)

God has not rejected Israel and the Jewish people. "The Seven" belong to them. Remember, Paul wrote: "...to whom belongs..." (Romans 9:4b)

Jealousy

Sadly, the church's track record has been as discouraging as Israel's biblical history. This is not only the case in the historic churches. This is also true of the early Church. Practically all of Paul's epistles were sent to churches that had difficulties with doctrine, practice and lifestyle. Only two out of seven churches addressed in Revelation (ch. 2-3) received a good report from the glorified Savior.[35] Five did not.[36] If the Church was graded, that is about a 30% approval rating.

However, along with corrections, indictments and warnings came promises and hope to each group and we rejoice in this: Jesus was speaking to them. Despite these rebukes, we hold to a high view of God's love for the Church and believe God will fulfill His ultimate purposes for the Church.

> All those I love, I rebuke and discipline. So be earnest and repent! Listen! I am standing at the door and knocking! If anyone hears my voice and opens the door I will come into his home and share a meal with him, and he with me. I will grant the one who conquers permission to sit with me on my throne, just as I too conquered and sat

> down with my Father on his throne (Revelation 3:19-21).

How high are the purposes of God for the Church? Amongst other things, Gentile believers apparently have the keys to unlocking the end times. The Church is called to fulfill the Great Commission and to provoke Israel to jealousy. The word translated "jealousy" (parazeloo), is typically defined like this:

The Church is called to fulfill the Great Commission and to provoke Israel to jealousy.

> to cause someone to feel strong jealousy or resentment against someone—to make jealous, to cause to be envious.[37]

This word is used three times in Romans:

> But I ask, did Israel not understand? First Moses says, "I will make you jealous (*parazeloo*) of those who are not a nation; with a foolish nation I will make you angry" (Romans 10:19).
>
> So, I ask, did they stumble in order that they might fall? By no means! Rather through their trespass salvation has come to the Gentiles, so as to make Israel jealous (*parazeloo*).
>
> Now if their trespass means riches for the world, and if their failure means riches for the Gentiles, how much more will their full inclusion mean!
>
> Now I am speaking to you Gentiles. Inasmuch then as I am an apostle to the Gentiles, I magnify my ministry in order somehow to make my fellow

> Jews jealous (*parazeloo*), and thus save some of them (Romans 11:11-14).

Israel, seeing the fullness of the life of the Messiah in the Church (Ephesians 1:23; 3:19; 4:13), will be provoked to turn to God through the Messiah. That is an incredible destiny. It inspires a tremendous amount of confidence in the ultimate state of the international believing community.

To come into this destiny, one thing from which the Church must be freed is the desire to rob Israel's inheritance.

To come into this destiny, one thing from which the Church must be freed is the desire to rob Israel's inheritance. Here's an awkward allegory.

First, the biblical passage:

> Now it came about, when Isaac was old and his eyes were too dim to see ...
>
> Then he came to his father and said, "My father." And he said, "Here I am. Who are you, my son?" Jacob said to his father, "I am Esau your firstborn; I have done as you told me. Get up, please, sit and eat of my game, that you may bless me."
>
> Isaac said to his son, "How is it that you have it so quickly, my son?" And he said, "Because the LORD your God caused it to happen to me."
>
> Then Isaac said to Jacob, "Please come close, that I may feel you, my son, whether you are really my son Esau or not." So Jacob came close to Isaac his father, and he felt him and said, "The voice is the

> voice of Jacob, but the hands are the hands of Esau."
>
> He did not recognize him, because his hands were hairy like his brother Esau's hands; so he blessed him. And he said, "Are you really my son Esau?" And he said, "I am" (Genesis 27:1a,18-24).

Now the allegory...

In the text, Jacob misrepresented himself as Esau to his father whose vision had grown "dim." Perhaps Isaac suffered from macular degeneration. In the "spiritual interpretation" I'm presenting, the Church, severed from all affectionate, functional and theological connection with the Jewish people, has presented itself to God as "Jacob" saying,

> *We are Israel. The Seven belong to us.*
>
> *After all, the spirit of adoption is upon the Church, the glory of God's presence is enjoyed in the Church. We Gentile believers partake of the New Covenant and are spiritual children of Abraham. We are the custodians of the Scriptures. We function as priesthood and temple.*
> *Therefore, the spiritual reality of the promises are ours and the Patriarchs have more in common with us than with the Jews...*
>
> *We are Israel.*

The Church, separating itself from the Jewish people, presents itself to God as the "firstborn." Does God suffer from macular degeneration? No. Neither is God senile. He remembers well the face of Israel. Does God reject those who so exalt themselves? No, but Father gently refers Gentile believers back to Paul's authoritative summation of Israel's identity. "The Seven" blessings still belong to the Jewish people.

When Paul wrote to Roman Gentile house-churches he called them to recognize and rejoice that God had lavished blessings upon and honored the entirety of the Jewish people. This was not to be viewed as having existed in their past. Rather, they are blessed and honored in their present.

Someday the Church will not be threatened by, or jealous of, God blessing and honoring Israel as the older brother, beloved of our Father.[38]

In that day, the Church will better understand the Scriptures and the heart of the Spirit of God who inspired the authors.[39] An interpretation of the apostolic doctrine that is influenced by a jealous, usurping spirit (traditional supersessionism) may produce the appearance of wisdom and insight, but it is actually adverse to the Kingdom of God.

> But if you have bitter jealousy and selfish ambition in your hearts, do not boast and be false to the truth. This is not the wisdom that comes down from above, but is earthly, unspiritual, demonic. For where jealousy and selfish ambition exist, there will be disorder and every vile practice (James 3:14-16).

Israel is precious in God's eyes. Therefore, He honored them and displayed His love for them. He still does. The degree of honor given is a measure of how precious and loved they are.

> Because you are precious in my eyes, and honored, and I love you, I give men in return for you, peoples in exchange for your life (Isaiah 43:4).

"The Seven" and the crowning honor of, "according to the flesh (Romans 9:5b)," being the people from whom the Messiah came "in the flesh" indicates the quality of the love with which God loves the Patriarchs' descendants. The honor of being the people through whom God would incarnate is awe provoking. It is a unique, eternally abiding, permanent honor. Nothing can happen that will diminish that honor. When we see this, and come into agreement with God about Israel's value, we open ourselves up for increased fellowship with the God of Abraham, Isaac, and Israel. May we judiciously apply Mary's theme to them, fulfilling the spirit behind this word:

When we come into agreement with God about Israel's value, we open ourselves up for increased fellowship with the God of Abraham, Isaac, and Israel. May we judiciously apply Mary's theme to them.

> For—imagine it!—from now on, all generations will call me blessed! (Luke 1:48b)

Let us be part of the generation that says,

> *"Yes, Lord. Israel is blessed.*
>
> *"They brought Jesus into the world.*
>
> *"What an honor, what a display of Your love, how amazing!*
>
> *"It is through them that You have loved us."*

When we're willing to see, our vision will be restored.

The Scripture says, "belongs," not "belonged". Paul was living in the present tense, grieved about the current state of his people while anticipating the future restoration.

To explore the nature of God's love for the Jewish people, utilize these sacred words as windows of revelation. Do you see what Paul saw? Read "The Seven" again.

> [They] are Israelites, to whom belongs
>
> the adoption as sons,
>
> and the glory
>
> and the covenants
>
> and the giving of the Law
>
> and the temple service
>
> and the promises,
>
> whose are the fathers,
>
> and from whom is the Christ according to the flesh, who is over all, God blessed forever. Amen (Romans 9:4-5).

That is how God honored Israel. He honors them to this day because He loves them and wants Israel to be honored by the Church.

Pray along those lines...

7

The Romans Framework

IN ROMANS, WE HAVE A THOROUGH EXPOSITION OF the gospel. We can also read some of the most poignant and passionate examples of Paul's self-disclosure. In addition, Paul consistently directs the reader's attention to verses from the prophetic writings of Israel. The extent of God's self-revelation referenced by Paul rivals the apostle's vulnerability. They are plainly written. They invite our hearts to open and summon our minds to meditate. In these sections, Paul not only reveals his own heart, but he also reveals God's heart.

The New Testament was not written in a vacuum. Each Gospel and letter, even the Apocalypse, was written to specific believing communities for specific purposes.

To uncover the apostles' testimony concerning God's love for the Jewish people—and His desire that His Church express this love—it is advantageous to carefully read Paul's letter to the house-churches in Rome with an open heart. Within Romans, Paul reveals the mysteries of Israel's election, estrangement, the role of the remnant, the promise of all Israel's reconciliation, and the glory accompanying the Jewish people's future restoration. It is in Romans that Jewish and Gentile disciples are instructed to honor one another. It is in Romans that Gentile

> *There is no better source of revelation concerning God's love for all Israel in the entire New Testament.*

believers are reminded to esteem the Jewish people. There is no better source of revelation concerning God's love for all Israel in the entire New Testament. In Romans, this is clearly explained. Why?

Why Was Romans Written?

In 1987 I was exposed to the understanding that Romans was written to bring about unity and mutual esteem between Gentile and Jewish believers in Jesus. It seems that variations of this theme have become the predominant, common understanding amongst current evangelical scholarship. Here is a concise summation of this view:

> Situation:
>
> Many of the founders of the Roman church were Jewish Christians (Acts 2:10). But sometime in the 40s A.D., the emperor Claudius, like the earlier emperor Tiberius, expelled the Jewish community from Rome (see Acts 18:2 and the Roman historians Suetonius and Dio Cassius). The Roman church was thus composed entirely of Gentiles until Claudius's death, when his edict was automatically repealed, and Jewish Christians returned to Rome (Rom 16:3). Jewish and Gentile Christians had different cultural ways of expressing their faith in Jesus; Paul thus must address a church experiencing tension between two valid cultural expressions of the Christian faith.[40]

I essentially agree. I would add that Paul was urgently anticipating the dawn of the coming age and, in the light of that hope, sought to prepare a people who would be ready for the Lord's return.

It is from within this highly charged eschatological context we find the foundational phrase:

> "...in regards the election (*their being chosen*), they are beloved for the sake of the patriarchs" (Romans 11:28b).

What does this mean? How is this love understood? What relevance does it have today?

Emotions in Romans 9:1-11:2

Paul's apostolic instruction was infused with prophetic emotion and insight. He was primarily a preacher, not a mere academic.[41] He was an apostle, not someone who constantly offered mere learned opinions.

> For this I was appointed a preacher and an apostle (I am telling the truth, I am not lying) as a teacher of the Gentiles in faith and truth (1 Timothy 2:7).

Yet, he reasoned with the Roman believers. In Romans 9-11 he relentlessly brought those who heard this letter to the common conclusion that "all Israel"[42] had an unfulfilled destiny. As he built his argument, he brought believers into an increased understanding of who God is and what He is like. As he taught on the relationship of Israel and the Church, Paul revealed God's emotions. What did he reveal about God's heart?

Love and Choice

Consider His love and choice. We begin our exploration of God's heart at the first specific description of God's emotions in these chapters:

> Just as it is written, "JACOB I LOVED, BUT ESAU I HATED" (Romans 9:13).

Here we find that God loved and called Jacob, but rejected Esau. This love is an emotion God felt so strongly that it motivated Him to act. He loved Jacob. He called Jacob. He not only wanted Jacob to be in a relationship with Himself, but He also loved Jacob for His redemptive purposes. (Anyone who does not believe that God also loved Esau and wanted Esau to be in a relationship with Him, misreads the text.)

Thus, Jacob was called to God, for God. This revelation indicates that God's love can be specific, particular, and prioritized. It was that way for Jacob.

Jacob was called to God, for God. This revelation indicates that God's love can be specific, particular, and prioritized.

It may be important to bring to mind that God was seeing the nation of Israel personified in Jacob as the Edomites were personified in Esau. In Jacob's case, He loved what He saw and chose him.

Mercy, Compassion, Judgment

Consider His mercy, compassion, and judgment. In Romans 9:15, we read,

> For He says to Moses, "I WILL HAVE MERCY ON WHOM I HAVE MERCY, AND I WILL HAVE COMPASSION ON WHOM I HAVE COMPASSION."

Paul wrote that God the Father is awesome, sovereign, displays mercy and compassion, but He is willing to judge and make His wrath known. Examine Romans 9:17-18:

> For the Scripture says to Pharaoh, "FOR THIS VERY PURPOSE I RAISED YOU UP, TO DEMONSTRATE MY POWER IN YOU, AND THAT MY NAME MIGHT BE PROCLAIMED THROUGHOUT THE WHOLE EARTH." So then He has mercy on whom He desires, and He hardens whom He desires (Romans 9:17-18).

God, moved with love, shows mercy and compassion. God, moved by the same love, is angry at wickedness and will reveal that as well. Some may regard Paul's depiction as a very "Old Testament" view of God, but, after all, Paul worshipped the God revealed in the Old Testament. That God became incarnate in Jesus.

Paul was evenhanded in his revelation of God's emotions. Love, demonstrated in intervention, blessing and fellowship is contrasted with a willingness to judge wickedness. He exercises judgment for the sake of revealing His delivering power which He always exercises for the sake of His beloved.

God has desires.

One desire He revealed is that He wants to make His power known. But why does He want His name to be known "throughout the earth?" For love's sake. He used His power to reveal His loving deliverance. God freely offers that saving power to the nations. The God of Israel desires to deliver them, too. They need to be saved, and He calls them to Himself. Isaiah relayed God's saving summons:

> Turn to Me and be saved, all the ends of the earth;
> For I am God, and there is no other (Isaiah 45:22).

> *God is not looking for His power to be admired. He is using His power to reveal His loving deliverance.*

He is not looking for His power to be admired. He is using His power to reveal His loving deliverance. God is offering that saving power to the nations. The God of Israel desires to be the God of the nations, too.

Patience, Perseverance

In addition to God's love, choice, mercy, compassion, and judgment, consider His patience and perseverance:

> What if God, although willing to demonstrate His wrath and to make His power known, endured with much patience vessels of wrath prepared for destruction? And He did so to make known the riches of His glory upon vessels of mercy... (Romans 9:22-23a)

The apostle wrote that God exercised patient endurance while putting up with rebellion (9:22-23a). Let's consider "patient endurance".

Patience is related to suffering. So, also, "endurance" reveals a willingness to go through a painful trial for something that you love. You do not "endure" what gives you pleasure, and the word "patience" is not normally used to describe fun. For the sake of the revelation of His goodness, He was willing to endure Egypt's ever increasing despotic, and ultimately genocidal, tyranny. God did not rejoice in the "vessels of wrath" perversely developing into that which needed to be destroyed.

God was committed to drawing nations to Himself through Israel. He endured evil's flourishing for the sake of contrasting His goodness and power. His glory and His goodness have been connected since the time of the Exodus. Here is some context for Paul's meditation:

> The LORD said to Moses, "I will also do this thing of which you have spoken; for you have found favor in My sight and I have known you by name."
>
> Then Moses said, "I pray You, show me Your glory!"
>
> And He said, "I Myself will make all My goodness pass before you, and will proclaim the name of the LORD before you; and I will be gracious to whom I will be gracious, and will show compassion on whom I will show compassion" (Exodus 33:17-19).

It is worth noting this unfolding of glory is a revelation of God's goodness.

Loving Jealousy, Helpless Entreating

Consider His loving jealousy.

Later in chapter 9, Paul reinforced the reality of God's emotions. God calls some, "beloved," a deeply affectionate term.

> As He says also in Hosea, "I WILL CALL THOSE WHO WERE NOT MY PEOPLE, 'MY PEOPLE,' AND HER WHO WAS NOT BELOVED, 'BELOVED'" (Romans 9:25).

Within the context of the Scriptures, "beloved" does not always have romantic connotations. However, within the context of Hosea, this word must have marital implications.

Furthermore, we find that He determined to make Israel

jealous through redeemed Gentiles.

> But I say, surely Israel did not know, did they? First Moses says, "I WILL MAKE YOU JEALOUS BY THAT WHICH IS NOT A NATION, BY A NATION WITHOUT UNDERSTANDING WILL I ANGER YOU" (Romans 10:19).

Why would one seek to make another jealous? What motive is revealed? There is an emotion implied behind this action: He longs for Israel's return. He desires to wake them up and win their affections. Paul represented Israel's husband as saying to the Jewish people, "It is not too late. Return to Me." God seeks to provoke Israel to jealousy. And then, to stress God's longing, two verses later Paul cites a poignant oracle:

> "ALL THE DAY LONG I HAVE STRETCHED OUT MY HANDS TO A DISOBEDIENT AND OBSTINATE PEOPLE" (Romans 10:21).

Look at this word-picture: "All the day long have I stretched out My hands..." What does that portray? To whom are they stretched? Is He reaching out? Is He pleading? What was the motive for stretching out His hands? Why does He do this?

It is a picture of omnipotence embracing helplessness. God is entreating Israel to return.

Here are two verses with the same Hebrew expression. When you read them, you will see this gesture conveys powerless desire.

> I stretch out my hands to You; My soul longs for You, as a parched land. Selah (Psalm 143:6).

> Zion stretches out her hands; There is no one to comfort her... (Lamentations 1:17a)

Here is an amazing revelation: God doesn't force anyone, but He can plead. And Paul reinforced the record that, according to Isaiah, at one time He did. Amazingly, Paul wrote that He has not stopped entreating, and the object of His consistent and unrelenting appeal is "to a disobedient and obstinate people."

The words "disobedient and obstinate" describe a relational and hierarchical relationship. They should obey, as He is their Father. They should cooperate; Israel should respond, for He is Lord. God is open to them. His hands are outstretched. God pleads with His people to return to Him.

Did Paul use this picture of outstretched hands to hint at a crucifixion? Surely, God's heart is pierced. This is a depiction of unrequited love, of an unreturned affection, of disappointment and hope against hope.

In this oracle, we do not find the language of a dispassionate theologian. Paul reiterated the passionate depths of prophetic revelation. He revealed to the Gentiles at Rome that Jehovah the Broken-hearted God is reduced to begging His beloved to come home.

Paul reiterated the passionate depths of prophetic revelation. He revealed to the Gentiles at Rome that Jehovah the Brokenhearted God is reduced to begging His beloved to come home.

As in the prophets Paul quoted, Israel is characterized as adamantly refusing to heed the call. God is calling; Israel refuses to hear. They refuse to come. As Israel rejected God in the days of Isaiah, so, in the days of Messiah, majority-Israel still rejects the God who longs for them. How then does the God of Abraham, Isaac and Jacob feel about being rejected? We find hints of this in Jeremiah and Hosea.

> "Behold, days are coming," declares the LORD, "when I will make a new covenant with the house of Israel and with the house of Judah, not like the covenant which I made with their fathers in the day I took them by the hand to bring them out of the land of Egypt, My covenant which they broke, although I was a husband to them," declares the LORD (Jeremiah 31:31-32).

> Then the LORD said to me, "Go again, love a woman who is loved by her husband, yet an adulteress, even as the LORD loves the sons of Israel, though they turn to other gods..." (Hosea 3:1a)

We learn from the prophetic testimony that God deeply feels the rejection of His people. This rejection provokes pain-filled jealousy. His jealousy motivates sorrow, rage, and a startling resolve to restore His beloved people to Himself. All of this is born of His love. The God of Abraham, Isaac and Jacob is not a mellow "spirit" who takes everything in stride and takes nothing personally. The One "who sees all things" is not distant and objective. He is jealous. His love is jealous.[43] He announced with mountain-shaking fiery thunder, "I am the LORD your God...You shall have no other gods before Me."[44] This insistence of exclusivity reveals the character of the scriptural God. He has not changed since His Incarnation. He shook the earth again at His Passion.

In the New Testament, His emotions are revealed to be just

as intense as they ever were. Actually, they are displayed in a way that makes them even more overwhelming. For instance, who would ever guess that God loved enough to become incarnate, embrace humiliation, and welcome a painful death to reconcile us to Himself? Indeed, that incarnate, crucified love was more than most of His own people could comprehend or accept.

So, in Romans 10:21 Paul wrote that God pleads by stretching out His hands to a disobedient and obstinate people, yet He is spurned. What is the result?

> I say then, God has not rejected His people, has He? May it never be! For I too am an Israelite, a descendant of Abraham, of the tribe of Benjamin. God has not rejected His people whom He foreknew (Romans 11:1-2a).

How does God react to this rejection? Is He petulant? "You reject Me? Fine...I reject you! So there!" In the next sentence (which begins the next chapter) Paul began to deal with the assumption that God, being rejected, rejects in turn. Romans 11 opens by interacting with the last verse of Romans 10 (v. 21), and there the apostle said that God has not rejected His people in turn (11:1-2).

Look at these three verses (10:21-11:2) without the (normally helpful) device of numerically organized chapters and verses.

> But as for Israel He says, "ALL THE DAY LONG I HAVE STRETCHED OUT MY HANDS TO A DISOBEDIENT AND OBSTINATE PEOPLE."
>
> I say then, God has not rejected His people, has He? May it never be! For I too am an Israelite, a descendant of Abraham, of the tribe of Benjamin.

> God has not rejected His people whom He foreknew.

Paul was adamant. God has not renounced His relationship to the Jewish people. He wrote that God refuses to reject Israel. The apostle expressed intense indignation at its very suggestion. Paul's emotional response ("May it never be!") revealed God's heart: Our God is indignant at this thought.

A proof Paul posed was the preservation of the remnant of Israel, the Jewish believers in Yeshua. He reminded the Gentile believers of the truth that, as in Elijah's day, the preservation of the remnant is the means God uses to preserve the nation.

What about "their rejection"?

Consider their rejection.

> *Wait! The text says, "For if their rejection..."*

Having established that God has definitely not discarded Israel, we come to this:

> For if their rejection is the reconciliation of the world, what will their acceptance be but life from the dead? (Romans 11:15)

Was Paul contradicting himself? No. He was being realistic.

Despite the sacred verdict that God has not rejected His people, this sentence takes for granted that there is a form of rejection experienced by majority-Israel right now. However, before bringing us into tacitly acknowledging that reality, Paul prepared his hearers with an emphatic denunciation of the notion that God would discard "His people." He laid a foundation to ensure that he would not be misunderstood by the Gentile Roman Christians.

God has not utterly, finally, completely and irrevocably thrust Israel aside. However, at this time, the judicial blindness[45] that afflicts Israel is a form of rejection. It is similar to this:

> I will go away and return to My place, until they acknowledge their guilt and seek My face; In their affliction they will earnestly seek Me (Hosea 5:15).

We are to understand that this is partial and temporal. When it comes to God's emotions, He cannot give Israel up.

> How can I give you up, O Ephraim? How can I surrender you, O Israel? How can I make you like Admah? How can I treat you like Zeboiim? My heart is turned over within Me, all My compassions are kindled.
>
> I will not execute My fierce anger; I will not destroy Ephraim again. For I am God and not man, the Holy One in your midst, and I will not come in wrath (Hosea 11:8-9).

Does Paul's instruction sound conflicted? Perhaps. But it is still a revelation consonant with the prophets that came before him. According to the prophetic testimony, there are aspects of God's heart that are deeply conflicted. His relationship to Israel (in fact, to all humanity) is a bit conflicted, but we know the outcome based on James 2:13b, "(M)ercy triumphs over judgment."

The Other Side of Fatherhood: Severe Transitional Chastisement

On the other hand, Paul taught that God acted in judgment against most of Israel, and this judgment is a fearsome thing. Let us examine this rejection mentioned:

> What then? What Israel is seeking, it has not obtained, but those who were chosen obtained it, and the rest were hardened; just as it is written, "GOD GAVE THEM A SPIRIT OF STUPOR, EYES TO SEE NOT AND EARS TO HEAR NOT, DOWN TO THIS VERY DAY" (Romans 11:7-8).

The biblical blueprint describing God's relationship to Israel and the Jewish people contains the pattern of chastisement and restoration. Consider these oracles:

> Yet in spite of this, when they are in the land of their enemies, I will not reject them, nor will I so abhor them as to destroy them, breaking My covenant with them; for I am the LORD their God (Leviticus 26:44).

> For the Lord will not reject forever (Lamentations 3:31).

> And I will bring them back, Because I have had compassion on them; And they will be as though I had not rejected them, For I am the LORD their God and I will answer them (Zechariah 10:6b).

Since the great majority of the Jewish people rejected God's work in the Messiah, why is there still a future for this nation? Why doesn't He cast Israel aside? What emotion is evidenced in this revelation? His refusal to completely reject manifests persistent longsuffering love.

> You are My servant, I have chosen you and not rejected you (Isaiah 41:9b).

If He does not reject Israel, what does He do? He punishes, preserves, and plans on His people's restoration. He patiently works towards that restoration. Why? What is His motive? His motive is love, and His love does not give up. Rather, love strengthens and motivates (1 Corinthians 13:8a; 8:1). Israel is the first nation to be called God's son. Within that context, God's chastisement is a manifestation of relationship.

If He does not reject Israel, what does He do? He punishes, preserves, and plans on His people's restoration.

> Then you shall say to Pharaoh, "Thus says the LORD, 'Israel is My son, My firstborn'" (Exodus 4:22).

> "FOR THOSE WHOM THE LORD LOVES HE DISCIPLINES, AND HE SCOURGES EVERY SON WHOM HE RECEIVES. It is for discipline that you endure; God deals with you as with sons; for what son is there whom his father does not discipline? But if you are without discipline, of which all have become partakers, then you are illegitimate children and not sons" (Hebrews 12:6-8).

One can see God the Father's disciplinary actions for individuals in the mirror of the God of Israel's relationship to His firstborn nation. This unique, prophetically proclaimed, public display of discipline and restoration is a demonstration of God's determination to restore His people to relational sonship.

In Romans 11:1 the phrase "His people" speaks of their

belonging to God. Israel is God's possession, something that is His from age to age; an everlasting inheritance. God lays claim to the Jewish people. They are His. In Deuteronomy 32:9 we read,

> For the LORD'S portion is His people; Jacob is the allotment of His inheritance.

I find it intriguing how Jeremiah turned this relationship around. Israel also has a "portion" and it is the One who has claimed them as His own inheritance. It is covenant; it is a marriage. God views His people as His portion and His people reciprocate.

> The portion of Jacob is not like these; for the Maker of all is He, and Israel is the tribe of His inheritance; the LORD of hosts is His name (Jeremiah 10:16).

Here is a summation of God's interaction with His people that may have informed Paul's theology:

> For the LORD will not abandon His people, nor will He forsake His inheritance (Psalm 94:14).

But is that fair?

Is it just that God should continue to be faithful to those who rejected Him? Is there nobody to speak up against this type of devotion? Is it right that God should be rejected and yet remain devoted to those who turned Him away? Who will stand up against God's foolish faithfulness on behalf of His best interests? Where is there a prophet who rightly comprehends the righteous consequences of Israel's rejection of the Son of God? Who loves God enough to denounce those who spurn His outstretched hands?

Elijah vs. Israel

In Romans 11:1-2, we found that that God calls disobedient Israel, "His people." This phrase is used about eighty times in Scripture to describe Israel's relationship to God. They belong to Him. He treasures them and will not reject them. He will not reject them even if His prophets cry out against them. Look at Paul's retelling of the story of Elijah's intercession against Israel.

> Or do you not know what the Scripture says in the passage about Elijah, how he pleads with God against Israel?
>
> "Lord, THEY HAVE KILLED YOUR PROPHETS, THEY HAVE TORN DOWN YOUR ALTARS, AND I ALONE AM LEFT, AND THEY ARE SEEKING MY LIFE."
>
> But what is the divine response to him? "I HAVE KEPT for Myself SEVEN THOUSAND MEN WHO HAVE NOT BOWED THE KNEE TO BAAL" (Romans 11:2b-4).

Elijah has been acknowledged as the archetypic prophet since Malachi's prophecy. This evaluation is confirmed by his appearance on the Mount of Transfiguration.[46]

Paul recorded that this quintessential prophet had reached the end of his rope concerning Israel. Perhaps this was the second time he brought a prophetic accusation before the court of heaven. The first time Elijah prayed, his prayer was effective. It produced a three-year drought (James 5:17-18). Paul described another time the prophet prayed against the covenant people. Notice, Paul wrote, "(Elijah) pleads with God against Israel" (Romans 11:2b).

That Elijah displayed a hostile attitude is not surprising. After all, Israel's establishment had killed the prophets. Perhaps many of them were his disciples. In addition, they (represented by their king and queen) were persecuting him. Finally, those with influence did nothing to stop this injustice. In response to Elijah's prayer on Carmel, God revealed Himself with fiery glory, yet Israel's royalty refused to repent. I believe Elijah's zeal for God was just as fiery, and he could not stand Israel's rejection of the God he loved.

Elijah had a case against Israel, and he determined to bring it before God's throne. He had reason to believe that he would be heard. God heard and answered his prayers before.

In the lawsuit, "Elijah vs. Israel", we observe a passionate prosecution of the northern kingdom (Romans 11:2). However, God rejected the prophet's case! He refused to hear it, threw it out of the heavenly court and determined to preserve Israel through the remnant. It was a "divine response."

Contrast Elijah's denunciation with Moses' intercession. In Exodus 32:10 we read that God was finished with the nation and intended to fulfill His covenant with the Patriarchs through Moses and his descendants.

> Now then let Me alone, that My anger may burn against them and that I may destroy them; and I will make of you a great nation (Exodus 32:10).

But in Exodus 32:12b-14, Moses pleaded with God to spare Israel:

> "Turn from Your burning anger and change Your mind about doing harm to Your people.

> Remember Abraham, Isaac, and Israel, Your servants to whom You swore by Yourself, and said to them, 'I will multiply your descendants as the stars of the heavens, and all this land of which I have spoken I will give to your descendants, and they shall inherit it forever.'"
>
> So the LORD changed His mind about the harm which He said He would do to His people.

In Romans, God is revealed as both loving defender and all-wise judge. In citing Elijah's example, Paul described something utterly different than the Exodus narrative. In fact, the roles are reversed. What a contrast! In Exodus, Israel is defended by Moses. But Paul portrayed Elijah as prosecuting God's people and the God of the people standing against the prophetic charge. Paul cited Elijah's complaint and God's reproof to drive home how God responds to those who would accuse Israel today. That dialog might look like this:

> *"God, reject Your people. They rejected You!"*
>
> *"No way! I shall preserve them through a faithful remnant and restore them at the end of this age."*

There is another time in the New Testament that Elijah's example of calling down heaven's judgment is referenced. In 2 Kings 1, Elijah's last prophetic act is recorded. Through His prophet, God revealed His supreme authority over the armies of men. King Ahaziah, son of Ahab, rejected Elijah's prophetic authority and judgment oracle. The apostate king sent a company of soldiers to arrest him, but Elijah did not go peacefully:

> And he said to him, "O man of God, the king says, 'Come down.'"

> Elijah replied to the captain of fifty, "If I am a man of God, let fire come down from heaven and consume you and your fifty."
>
> Then fire came down from heaven and consumed him and his fifty (2 Kings 1:9-10).

When Jesus was rejected in Samaria, His disciples, in an eruption of unsanctified loyalty, wanted to do an Elijah imitation:

> He sent messengers on ahead of Him, and they went and entered a village of the Samaritans to make arrangements for Him. But they did not receive Him, because He was traveling toward Jerusalem. When His disciples James and John saw this, they said, "Lord, do You want us to command fire to come down from heaven and consume them?" (Luke 9:52-54)

The next verse recorded how Jesus rebuked His disciples (Luke 9:55).

The perspective Paul corrected could have been held by Gentile or Jewish believers in Jesus and expressed like this:

> *Surely, majority-Israel is no longer worthy of calling, gifts, or promise.*

This view can be held by people who are zealous for God's glory and are incredulous that most of the Jewish people rejected the Messiah. In addition, in Paul's time, as in Elijah's day,

> *It turns out that God is not prosecuting His people. Rather than reacting out of wounded, jealous rage, God stands up for Israel.*

the prophetic remnant of Israel was persecuted by a powerful, unfaithful establishment.

However, in spite of the Elijah-like perspective that Israel is no longer worthy of either gifts or calling, it turns out that God is not prosecuting His people. Paul's letter reminds us that rather than reacting out of wounded, jealous rage, God stands up for Israel. He withstands even the holy accuser (Elijah, and those like him). He works with a remnant to preserve the whole.

Concerning God's emotions: one preserves and defends what one loves. God is lovingly protective of Israel. He rejects the adversary's case.

> The LORD said to Satan, "The LORD rebuke you, Satan! Indeed, the LORD who has chosen Jerusalem rebuke you!" (Zechariah 3:2a)

Meanwhile, God is not a co-dependent pushover. Due to majority-Israel's rejection of the Messiah the Jewish people are experiencing the absence of His protective presence and are subject to divine resistance. This resistance is seen in the horror of experiencing what the pagan world experiences: the hardening of heart, and being given over to their own desires. In this case, since Israel refuses to see that Jesus is the Messiah, they are given over to a form of spiritual blindness. But this blindness is not the whole story. God will not abandon His people. In the rest of Romans 11, Paul provided an outline of Israel's current story and destiny. Ultimately, the saga's surprise ending is set forth for all to see.

> *This blindness is not the whole story. God will not abandon His people.*

Judged, But Not Rejected

Romans 11 is clear that they were judged. Look at this profound declaration of temporal wrath:

> Just as it is written, "GOD GAVE THEM A SPIRIT OF STUPOR, EYES TO SEE NOT AND EARS TO HEAR NOT, DOWN TO THIS VERY DAY."
>
> And David says, "LET THEIR TABLE BECOME A SNARE AND A TRAP, AND A STUMBLING BLOCK AND A RETRIBUTION TO THEM. LET THEIR EYES BE DARKENED TO SEE NOT, AND BEND THEIR BACKS FOREVER" (Romans 11:8-10).

Paul taught that although God had not rejected Israel, He did specifically, and uniquely, chastise His people. He did this in a way that is according to the covenant pattern revealed in the Torah and Prophets. This righteous judgment has come to pass due to the rejection of the Messiah by the majority of the Jewish people. We do not know if there is another nation that is likewise judged in relationship to their faith in the Messiah. The Bible is silent about that. The only people group revealed through the Scriptures as being under this type of curse is Paul's kinsmen (Romans 9:3). Remember, he referred to them as God's people (Romans 11:2).

These verses in Romans 11:8-10 are a frightening demonstration of strategically controlled severity. Taken out of context, we would think they would signify the permanent end of Israel's relationship to God: "bend their backs forever." However, in this chapter, it is revealed that behind the scenes God is heartbroken and jealous of His people's affection and loyalty. Due to this jealousy, He determined to fulfill another prophecy and make Israel jealous of His affection and interaction.

We read about His plan here:

> I say then, they did not stumble so as to fall, did they? May it never be! But by their transgression salvation has come to the Gentiles, to make them jealous (Romans 11:11).

Recapitulate:

God loved and chose Jacob.

His heart is tender, manifesting itself in mercy and compassion. God's heart perseveringly loves with divine longsuffering. He endures the growth of evil until it can no longer be ignored. This is described as "patient endurance."

He executes judgment on satanic wickedness and reveals His goodness to both those afflicted by cruel tyranny (the Exodus), and those nations who become aware of that deliverance.

God experiences jealousy, along with brokenhearted, unrequited love.

In that emotional state, He acts to turn the tables and provoke Israel to jealousy so that they would return to Him.

His heart cries out for Israel. If He were corporeal, we would see a heartbroken man pleading with the one who rejected Him to return.

God also remains fiercely loyal to those who have abandoned Him. They are still His people. Although He feels the rejection, He does not utterly repudiate Israel. Not only does He not reject Israel, but He preserves them through saving a remnant.

Surprisingly, God stands up for His people against the accusations brought against them. He protects them in heaven's court.

Ultimately, due to His amazing intervention, Israel will be utterly reconciled to Himself. This will release the fullness of the Kingdom's manifestation of God's delight.

Paul revealed that God's feelings concerning His people span the entire spectrum of emotions.

Finally:

Those called to intercede on God's behalf are not called to denounce Israel before the throne. God is looking for people to fellowship with Him in prayer for the preservation of Israel's remnant, and that the Church primarily comprised of redeemed Gentiles would fulfill their calling to make His people jealous.

To what degree does He love His people? He revealed through Paul that Isaiah's prophecy revealing God's unrequited love would be a heart-piercing, relevant message to the Church throughout the ages.

Embrace that oracle.

Pray for God's heart to be satisfied.

May all His good purposes for His people be established in our generation.

8

God's Anticipation: Reconciliation in Romans 11

Some Background:

HERE IS A KEY VERSE THAT DESCRIBES THE realization of end-time fullness. It poses a rhetorical question that demands an honest answer.

> For if their rejection is the reconciliation of the world, what will their acceptance be but life from the dead? (Romans 11:15)

I have noticed that, often, only a part of the first clause of 11:15 is cited: "...their rejection is the reconciliation of the world." For those who have their identity wrapped up in being the "New True Israel" the rest of the sentence may be challenging. The second part of Paul's question, "What will their acceptance be but life from the dead?", is regularly ignored. This is similar to what usually happens when Romans 1:16 is cited. It is generally quoted:

> For I am not ashamed of the gospel, for it is the power of God for salvation to everyone who believes (Romans 1:16a).

I have found that it is unusual for the whole of Romans 1:16 to be quoted. Here is the entire sentence:

> For I am not ashamed of the gospel, for it is the power of God for salvation to everyone who believes, to the Jew first and also to the Greek.

Once again, the Bible is selectively quoted because of theological convenience or through minimizing the import of the entire thought. From my perspective, these two similar omissions point to a common bias.

The Church tends to reject or minimize Paul's revelation about the sovereignly ordained place of the Jewish people in the preaching of the gospel (Rom. 1:16). In the same way, the Church tends to ignore or minimize Israel's role in the restoration of the world (Rom. 11:15).

Contrasted with the church's historic antagonism, or apathy, in Romans 11:15 we find a description of Paul's fervent conviction concerning the end-times. His hope is relevant to our exploration of God's heart. The Apostle Paul represented God. Therefore, this verse is important for our discussion of a New Testament view of God's love for the Jewish people.

Relevance to God's Heart

Here's a general rule: when we encounter a verse that states the outcome of something God wants to happen, we should dignify it and see it as a revelation of His desires. He has emotions. In this case, it is revealed that He wants Israel's reconciliation to happen, is working towards that reality, and is waiting for His plan to be realized. God longs for Israel's return to Himself. His yearning stirs Him to action. His anticipation is an emotion. The God of Abraham, Isaac, and Jacob feels anticipation as well as determination, which produces perseverance. He is going to make this happen as the Body of the Messiah co-labors with Him.

In Luke 15 we find three parables that end with celebrations: the lost sheep, the lost coin and the lost son. In each instance, the finder calls friends and family to join in a festive expression of joy. When the woman found her coin and when the shepherd found his sheep, they said, "Rejoice with me, for I have found..." (Luke 15:6b, 9b) These verses provide pictures of heaven's joy.

Here is the point Jesus was making:

> I tell you that in the same way, there will be more joy in heaven over one sinner who repents than over ninety-nine righteous persons who need no repentance...I tell you, there is joy in the presence of the angels of God over one sinner who repents (Luke 15:7-10b).

In the parable of the Return of the Lost Son, the pattern continued and expanded. The Scripture gives this simile:

> "Let us eat and celebrate; for this son of mine was dead and has come to life again; he was lost and has been found." And they began to celebrate (Luke 15:23b-24).

> *If heaven rejoices over the repentance of a single individual, then what of an entire nation?*

If heaven rejoices over the repentance of a single individual, then what of an entire nation? Imagine God's rejoicing over Israel's return at the end of this age. This reconciliation will delight God to the degree that He will call for the ultimate party.

There are biblical foretellings likening the results of Israel's restoration to an extravagant celebration. The most famous metaphor is the feast described in Revelation 19:9:

> Then he said to me, "Write, 'Blessed are those who are invited to the marriage supper of the Lamb.'" And he said to me, "These are true words of God" (Revelation 19:9).

This supper speaks of heightened supernatural joy. And consider this allegorical foreshadowing.

> "He has brought me to his banquet hall (*house of wine*), and his banner over me is love" (Song of Solomon 2:4).

The "marriage supper" hearkens back to the promise of "a lavish banquet" prophesied by Isaiah.

> The LORD of hosts will prepare a lavish banquet for all peoples on this mountain; a banquet of aged wine, choice pieces with marrow, and refined, aged wine. And on this mountain He will swallow up the covering which is over all peoples, even the veil which is stretched over all nations. He will swallow up death for all time, and the Lord GOD will wipe tears away from all faces, and He will remove the reproach of His people from all the earth; for the LORD has spoken (Isaiah 25:6-8).

This "lavish banquet" is a transnational celebration of humanity's liberation from death. Please note in Isaiah 25:8 the reference to death's destruction is connected to the removal of Israel's international reproach. What a prophecy! Did Paul know it? Of course he did, and he wrote of "life from the dead" (Romans 11:15b). Look at where Paul reiterated the end-time victory over the last enemy found in Isaiah 25:

> But when this perishable will have put on the imperishable, and this mortal will have put on immortality, then will come about the saying that is written, "DEATH IS SWALLOWED UP in victory" (1 Corinthians 15:54).

Paul reinforced the revelation that God views death as an enemy (1 Corinthians 15:25-26). The Lord of every Angel Army is an awesome warrior who is implacably opposed to death. Do you think Father is looking forward to the ultimate victory? Yes, He is. There is anticipation in the courts of heaven that proceeds from the throne. That expectancy will be fulfilled when Israel is reconciled to God.

> What will their acceptance be but life from the dead? (Romans 11:15b)

Take another look at the parable-party for the Prodigal Son. When Israel as "National Prodigal Son" returns, Father will call for a feast. Any objections? There may be many, but God has an answer for them.

> "Your brother has come, and your father has killed the fattened calf because he has received him back safe and sound." But he became angry and was not willing to go in; and his father came out and began pleading with him. But he answered and said to his father, "Look! For so many years I have been serving you and I have never neglected a command of yours; and yet you have never given me a young goat, so that I might celebrate with my friends; but when this son of yours came, who has devoured your wealth with prostitutes, you killed the fattened calf for him." And he said to him, "Son, you have always been with me, and all that is mine is yours. But we had to celebrate and rejoice, for this brother of yours was dead and has begun to live, and was lost and has been found" (Luke 15:27b-32).

To Gentile believers who may feel disinclined to participate in the celebration, which is the commencement of the age-to-come, God may say something like,

> *Look, I love you, but I have really, really, really been looking forward to Israel's return. Rejoice with Me. They are coming home!*

It takes believers who are emotionally secure in their identity to join Jesus in His anticipation over Israel's reconciliation. God has determined to connect His beloved people's restoration to that which will benefit all creation and every nation. He wants believers from the nations to fellowship with Him in this hope.

God Perseveres

The nations are now included in Israel's calling for Israel's sake. As Paul transitioned to the completion of his instruction concerning Israel, he instructed Gentile Christians about how to relate to their brethren, the Jewish believers. He included revelation about the Gentile believers' relationship to Jewish people who were yet unbelieving. He primarily did this through the metaphor of the olive tree.

> But if some of the branches were broken off, and you, being a wild olive, were grafted in among them and became partaker with them of the rich root of the olive tree, do not be arrogant toward the branches; but if you are arrogant, remember that it is not you who supports the root, but the root supports you.
>
> You will say then, "Branches were broken off so that I might be grafted in." Quite right, they were broken off for their unbelief, but you stand by your faith. Do not be conceited, but fear; for if God did not spare the natural branches, He will not spare you, either.
>
> Behold then the kindness and severity of God; to those who fell, severity, but to you, God's kindness, if you continue in His kindness; otherwise you also will be cut off. And they also, if they do not continue in their unbelief, will be grafted in, for God is able to graft them in again (Romans 11:17-23).

In Romans 11:17-23 there are some difficult truths. It speaks of unbelieving Jewish people being likened to severed branches and of Gentiles, represented by uncultivated olive branches, becoming part of this cultivated tree. It also rebukes the tendency towards anti-Semitic arrogance that was part of the Greco-Roman cultural mainstream. Paul wrote that Jewish people were broken off so Gentiles may fully participate in the life of the tree, and he warned the Gentile "branches" to not take this unlikely transfer for granted. Finally, Paul wrote that ultimately the broken-off branches could be grafted into the tree, again.

Paul wrote that ultimately the broken-off branches could be grafted into the tree again.

We're going to look at the role the redeemed of all nations have in fulfilling the ultimate purposes of the Kingdom. Their participation in the Kingdom's advance has its origin in God's heart. Like much that manifests the Kingdom, it is both a goal and part of a process at the same time. These who are carrying the word of reconciliation are both the objects of restoration and a means to Israel fulfilling its destiny. God loves Israel so much that He has called the nations to participate in the Jewish people's restoration.

Since there have been nations...

Here is some background to the inclusion of the Gentiles in this aspect of God's plan. First of all, God's original purpose was to bring the nations to Himself through blessing Israel. This prophetic hope was seen in promise, prayer, and prophecy.

> And in you all the families of the earth will be blessed (Genesis 12:3b).

> God be gracious to us and bless us, And cause His face to shine upon us-- Selah. That Your way may

> be known on the earth, Your salvation among all nations (Psalm 67:1-2).

> For behold, darkness will cover the earth and deep darkness the peoples; but the LORD will rise upon you and His glory will appear upon you. Nations will come to your light, and kings to the brightness of your rising (Isaiah 60:2-3).

The division of humanity into nations began after the rebellion known as "The Tower of Babel."

> So the LORD scattered them abroad from there over the face of the whole earth; and they stopped building the city. Therefore its name was called Babel, because there the LORD confused the language of the whole earth; and from there the LORD scattered them abroad over the face of the whole earth (Genesis 11:8-9).

Abram was called in the context of the inability of the nations to understand one another. Humanity was alienated from God *and* one another. This alienation was never intended to be permanent. God has always been motivated to reconcile them to Himself and one another. In Genesis 12, it is revealed that through God's blessing of Abram and his descendants, all nations could enter the experience of God's favor.

> Now the LORD said to Abram, "Go forth from your country, and from your relatives and from your father's house, to the land which I will show you; and I will make you a great nation, and I will bless you, and make your name great; and so you shall be a blessing; and I will bless those who bless you, and the one who curses you I will curse. And in you all the families of the earth will be blessed" (Genesis 12:1-3).

It was prophesied in the Psalms that all the nations would worship the God of Israel.

> All nations whom You have made shall come and worship before You, O Lord, and they shall glorify Your name (Psalm 86:9).

However, something that was not written is that godly Gentiles would be one of God's primary means to accomplish this transnational reconciliation. From the time of Abraham's calling to the outpouring of the Spirit upon Cornelius' household (Acts 10), this was understood to be Israel's job. Specifically, this was the task of Israel's godly remnant. In Romans, it is plainly revealed that now Gentile believers in Israel's Messiah share the same dignity and calling as the Jewish remnant. Justified, regenerated, Holy Spirit-filled Gentiles are more than the targets of remnant Israel's mission. These Gentile disciples have become active and vital participants in the advancement of the Kingdom. Paul likened these Gentile believers to wild olive branches that have been grafted into Israel's cultivated olive tree. These branches have borne fruit and are destined to be fruitful.

> *God is not thwarted; neither is He unfaithful.*

With the rejection of the Messiah, God's plan to co-labor with *all* Israel paused. However, God's determination to bring humanity to Himself did not stop. God is not thwarted; neither is He unfaithful. Majority-Israel's rejection of the Messiah was such a radical turn of events that the ancient warnings of Torah took on a fuller meaning. It was written in sacred oracle that God would make Israel jealous by a nation that was without understanding:

> So I will make them jealous with those who are not a people; I will provoke them to anger with a foolish nation (Deuteronomy 32:21b).

The Apostle Paul saw in Moses' warning a prophecy of God's work through the Church amongst the nations. Paul proclaimed that this process was beginning through Gentile believers in the Jewish Messiah.

> But I say, surely Israel did not know, did they? First Moses says, "I WILL MAKE YOU JEALOUS BY THAT WHICH IS NOT A NATION, BY A NATION WITHOUT UNDERSTANDING WILL I ANGER YOU" (Romans 10:19).

The expected end (jealousy) was further explained in the context of promise (restoration):

> I say then, they did not stumble so as to fall, did they? May it never be! But by their transgression salvation has come to the Gentiles, to make them jealous. Now if their transgression is riches for the world and their failure is riches for the Gentiles, how much more will their fulfillment be! (Romans 11:11-12)

This is a big part of Paul's explanation for the phenomenon of Gentiles being included in the Church: the locus of the Kingdom of God's reconciling activity in this age. This is a primary Pauline development of the narrative found in the Hebrew Scriptures. Some might accusingly say it is a divergence from what was plainly written. But, Paul called it a mystery.

> ...to be specific, that the Gentiles are fellow heirs and fellow members of the body, and fellow partakers of the promise in the Messiah Jesus through the gospel (Ephesians 3:6).

Concerning God's purposes with Israel, there is an aspect of "success" in the midst of the unhappiness of all that transpired.[47] After all, the totality of Israel is represented in God's anointed King, Jesus. Yeshua is the head and representative of the Jewish people. From His birth to his death, Jesus was prophetically identified as Israel's king.

> "Where is He who has been born King of the Jews? For we saw His star in the east and have come to worship Him" (Matthew 2:2).

> And above His head they put up the charge against Him which read, "THIS IS JESUS THE KING OF THE JEWS" (Matthew 27:37).

In addition, the principal players of the primitive Church were comprised of Jewish believers, Israel's godly apostolic remnant. The snowball of the nations' reconciliation to the one true God began with them. Remember, Paul was not the source of the revelation of God's determination to bring the nations to Himself. This is part of the testimony of the Hebrew Scriptures. What is astounding, and specifically a Pauline outlook, is that this was no longer an exclusively Jewish mission. God would now accomplish the reconciliation of the nations through Gentiles who were "grafted in among" (Romans 11:17b) the Jewish believers.

> But if some of the branches were broken off, and you, being a wild olive, were grafted in among them and became partaker with them of the rich root of the olive tree... (Romans 11:17)

One aspect of a healthy olive tree branch is that it produces more than leaves. People plant and cultivate olive trees to get olives. The branches, receiving life through God's olive tree, are destined to bear fruit. These "wild olive branches"[48] would have the same relationship, rights and responsibilities as Israel's remnant. Not only that, but they would experience the same affection and covenant attention from God as the faithful Jewish believers in Jesus.[49] They are included in the joyous outcome of all God's Kingdom purposes. They are those called by God to make Israel jealous. One reason for jealousy is this: Gentile believers are doing Israel's job.

What Paul appears to say is that God was resolved to reconcile the nations to Himself. He determined to bring His purpose to pass even if His primary strategy (to bless a fully restored national Israel in their own land) could no longer be fully operative. He decided to act even if it meant bypassing the majority of the people of Israel. Insofar as being the means of drawing the nations to God, at this time, the majority of Israel is disqualified. Suspending His ancient strategy, God is bringing the nations into a relationship with Himself through Israel's rejected King and Israel's despised remnant, the pre-70 A.D. believers and the Jewish believers who have followed them.

The "olive tree" into which believing Gentiles are grafted is not only relational and covenantal, it is also missional. Israel's mission to know, represent and proclaim God is now carried out, not only by the remnant of Israel (in particular, the foundational pre-70 A.D. apostolic company), but also by Gentiles who believe. This mission will continue until Israel's ultimate restoration brings about an even greater blessing than the results of their rejection.

The "olive tree" into which believing Gentiles are grafted is not only relational and covenantal, it is also missional.

> Now if their transgression is riches for the world and their failure is riches for the Gentiles, how much more will their fulfillment be! (Romans 11:12)

The Scriptures teach that, together with Israel, the nations were always the objects of God's desire. Paul revealed that now non-Jewish believers are included in the undertaking of reconciling the nations. This is big. At the same time as the apostle prophesied Israel's glorious prophetic destiny, he built up the self-worth of the Gentile believers. Paul made sure that Gentile believers knew the nations are not God's "second choice." Israel's election (after the Tower of Babel) was part of a strategic plan to bring alienated humanity, dead in their sins, cut off from covenant and God, back to the Father. Now in the light of majority-Israel's failure, the Gentile believers are brought into a higher status than was once available. They partake of the same calling as God's chosen people. They do this along with Israel's godly remnant who live up to the expectations of God's heart.

God always intended for the Gentiles to come into a relationship with Himself through His people. Israel was to be His advertisement. Through His manifestly blessing them, other nations would be drawn to God. Here's a succinct summation of the vision:

> God blesses us, that all the ends of the earth may fear Him (Psalm 67:7).

However, as far as I can see, He never promised, nor was it ever prophesied, that the nations would be a source of mission to the rest of the world. There may have been individual Gentiles who participated in God's missional plan. Surely there were God-fearers who gathered with their households (Acts 10:24). Also, remember, before Abraham, Isaac and Jacob's election there was no such thing as Israel. There was a godly antediluvian line that culminated in Noah, a preacher of righteousness, and his sons.

However, I cannot find biblical evidence for a concerted effort by Gentile believers to evangelize before Acts. Consider this incongruity: Gentile messengers, who are faithful to and sent by their Creator, who self-identifies as

Israel's God. That is such a strange idea. Yet, this is what happened and is continuing to increase.

Israel was intended to be a synergy of people and place (Land) that would draw Gentiles to the Almighty. This plan, apparently, is on hold, but the outreach to the nations is going full-speed ahead. Now, the nations are not coming, those partaking of the New Covenant are going. Surely it would have been enough for such wild branches to partake of the life of Israel's olive tree. Yet, beyond all expectations God had more in store. They do not just partake of "life," they are living "the life." They bear fruit. The believing remnants of the nations are bringing about the reconciliation of the nations until the fullness of the Gentiles comes in.

Majority-Israel failed to respond to Jesus and bring the nations into the Kingdom, but God decided to act anyway. He is acting through the very nations who, until they responded to the gospel, had no covenantal relationship to Himself or His people, Israel (Ephesians 2:11-13; 3:6).

> And Isaiah is very bold and says, "I WAS FOUND BY THOSE WHO DID NOT SEEK ME, I BECAME MANIFEST TO THOSE WHO DID NOT ASK FOR ME" (Romans 10:20).

The God of Abraham, Isaac and Jacob reserves the timing of the full manifestation of the age-to-come to follow Israel's national restoration. Israel's reconciliation is something we are encouraged to anticipate. However, as glorious as that will be, it is not an end in itself. It is a means to the purpose of Israel's original election.

> For the earth will be filled with the knowledge of the glory of the LORD, as the waters cover the sea (Habakkuk 2:14).

Yes, majority-Israel has temporarily rejected the Messiah and, in turn, suffered a similar rejection. However, this rejection is not final; it is temporary. Israel will be restored and through that restoration will come to pass God's greater goal: "life from the dead" (Romans 11:15b). God loved the nations and chose Israel to draw them to Himself. In similar manner, God's love for Israel is revealed through His choosing Gentile believers who are called to Himself and to mission. They are destined to help bring about Israel's national reconciliation. Their faithfulness is the way God has chosen to provoke majority-Israel to jealousy. This jealousy shall bring about Israel's reconciliation. Israel's restoration will bring about the fullness of the Kingdom.

> For just as you once were disobedient to God, but now have been shown mercy because of their disobedience, so these also now have been disobedient, that because of the mercy shown to you they also may now be shown mercy. For God has shut up all in disobedience so that He may show mercy to all.
>
> Oh, the depth of the riches both of the wisdom and knowledge of God! How unsearchable are His judgments and unfathomable His ways! For WHO HAS KNOWN THE MIND OF THE LORD, OR WHO BECAME HIS COUNSELOR? Or WHO HAS FIRST GIVEN TO HIM THAT IT MIGHT BE PAID BACK TO HIM AGAIN? For from Him and through Him and to Him are all things. To Him be the glory forever. Amen (Romans 11:30-36).

Kindness and Severity

Let us look a bit more at Paul's report concerning God's emotions. He wrote:

> Behold then the kindness and severity of God; to those who fell, severity, but to you, God's

> kindness, if you continue in His kindness; otherwise you also will be cut off (Romans 11:22).

We should pay attention to "kindness and severity." I cannot think of any other passages in the New Testament that reveal and contrast these two emotions and their consequences. When one's heart is hardened towards another, one is more inclined to cut the other person off. When one is filled with love, kindness results. God was emotionally affected by majority-Israel's rejection of His Son. To pretend that somehow God was "above it all," and Israel's disaffection could not reach Him, is to replace the scriptural God with something out of a philosopher's handbook. God-Impassible? Impossible. That is not the God who loved enough to become incarnate.

To pretend that somehow God was "above it all," and Israel's disaffection could not reach Him, is to replace the scriptural God with something out of a philosopher's handbook. God-Impassible? Impossible. That is not the God who loved enough to become incarnate.

The word "severity" describes harshness. It has the inference of abruptly cutting someone off. It describes the "cutting off" of those who "fell." And yet God's kindness remains, and the time of severity towards Israel will come to a permanent end.

> For I do not want you, brethren, to be uninformed of this mystery—so that you will not be wise in your own estimation—that a partial hardening has happened to Israel until the fullness of the Gentiles has come in; and so all Israel will be saved; just as it is written, "THE DELIVERER WILL COME FROM ZION, HE WILL REMOVE UNGODLINESS FROM JACOB." "THIS IS MY COVENANT WITH THEM, WHEN I TAKE AWAY THEIR SINS" (Romans 11:25-27).

Once again let us note that this will be the cause of great celebration.

> Oh, that the salvation of Israel would come out of Zion! When the LORD restores His captive people, Jacob will rejoice, Israel will be glad (Psalm 14:7).

Paul looked forward to the fulfilling of what he affirmed. The Church is called to share his anticipation. It reflects God's heart.

Irrevocably Called, Gifted, Chosen, Beloved, Enemies

Here is an amazing sentence that sums up much of what Paul wanted the Gentile believers to know about the Jewish people:

> From the standpoint of the gospel they are enemies for your sake, but from the standpoint of God's choice they are beloved for the sake of the fathers; for the gifts and the calling of God are irrevocable (Romans 11:28-29).

The people of Israel are described as irrevocably called, gifted, chosen, beloved *and* enemies. What a violent contrast: enemies and loved ones (Romans 11:28). How can these descriptions coexist? It is necessary to walk gently into this revelation. Take a deep breath, and let's go into the next chapter!

9

Enemies For Your Sake?

Paul summed up what he had written thus far in 11:28:

> From the standpoint of the gospel they are enemies for your sake, but from the standpoint of God's choice they are beloved for the sake of the fathers; for the gifts and the calling of God are irrevocable (Romans 11:28-29).

He minced no words here. Also, he did not tell the reader what the object of Israel's enmity is. It is not unreasonable to apply Romans 5, verses 8 and 10 to Israel's condition. After all, the Jewish people not only share the human condition, as a prophetic picture they exemplify humanity's plight.

> But God demonstrates His own love toward us, in that while we were yet sinners, (the Messiah) died for us...For if while we were enemies we were reconciled to God through the death of His Son, much more, having been reconciled, we shall be saved by His life (Romans 5:8, 10).

Certainly, they were enemies of God's kind intentions towards them as manifest in the gospel.

> But the Pharisees and the lawyers rejected God's purpose for themselves, not having been baptized by John (Luke 7:30).

Perhaps Paul was reporting that, within the context of the church at Rome, the non-believing Jewish community was at enmity with the message of Jesus. Therefore, they were enemies of the spread of the good news amongst the

Gentiles (to whom Paul was writing in Romans 11:28-29) and therefore, the community of gospel-preaching believers.

It is worth noting that, at times, Paul's ministry to the Gentiles was actively hindered by some Yeshua-rejecting Jewish leaders. Paul and his team wrote of this frustration and the subsequent indictment in a letter to the Thessalonians. Paul wrote:

> They are not pleasing to God, but hostile to all men, hindering us from speaking to the Gentiles so that they may be saved; with the result that they always fill up the measure of their sins. But wrath has come upon them to the utmost (1 Thessalonians 2:15-16).

What could possibly be the background to this statement? Perhaps we find it in Acts 17. In that chapter, we find that after some small initial success there was a nonbelieving, Jewish-inspired riot against the apostles in Thessalonica. When Paul and company went to nearby Berea, these same people followed them and stirred up trouble again. 1 Thessalonians 2 was written in the immediate light of these circumstances.

Perhaps Paul was drawing upon these types of situations when he wrote "they are enemies for your sake." It is true that believing Gentiles now had an opportunity to participate in the life and mission which had been reserved specifically and uniquely for Israel. This is a high privilege. Is that what Paul intended to say? There are differences of opinion concerning Paul's intent. However, what is certain is that, somehow, Jewish opposition to the preaching of the gospel to the Gentiles was working out for the benefit of those Gentiles who believed.

Of necessity, Paul had to embrace heartbreak and give his emotions no quarter as he determined to ruthlessly describe his beloved people Israel as an "enemy." After all, the apostle's testimony was that he would willingly endure eternal alienation from God for the sake of the Jewish people's reconciliation. So, if Paul was heartbroken over this state of affairs, what about God and His response? As we trace God's emotions, answer this question, "Is God Israel's enemy?" I'm sure that question would elicit another "God forbid!" from Paul. Despite majority-Israel's adverse attitude, God is not Israel's enemy. In fact, God loves the Jewish people. They are "beloved."

Despite majority-Israel's adverse attitude, God is not Israel's enemy. In fact, God loves the Jewish people. They are "beloved."

Beloved

> ...from the standpoint of God's choice, they are beloved for the sake of the fathers; for the gifts and the calling of God are irrevocable (Romans 11:28b-29).

Paul made a contrasting, unexpected, crystal clear statement: "according to the election, beloved for the sake of the Patriarchs." Here we have an unambiguous description of God's emotions towards the whole of Israel, not just the godly Yeshua-faithful remnant. How do we know this is about all of Israel and not just the remnant? Paul is writing about the same people he described as "enemies" for the sake of the Gentile believers.

These "enemies" are still "chosen" because they are "loved for the sake of the fathers."

These "enemies" are still "chosen" because they are "loved for the sake of the fathers."

This statement is powerful, lucid and unique to the New Testament writings. What a summation of the conflict between God and His people! What is the opposite of rejection? It is choice. Israel has not been rejected; they are chosen to this very day. What emotion lies behind choice? It is part of the Biblical perspective that God is often motivated by love for that which is outside Himself. That is a major truth we find in Romans 9-11. From the beginning of this section, the reader finds that God's determination to act and interact is predicated on His love.

> Just as it is written, "JACOB I LOVED, BUT ESAU I HATED" (Romans 9:13a).

No Regrets

> The gifts and the calling of God are irrevocable (Romans 11:29).

In the same sentence (Romans 11:28-29) we find a further description of the Jewish people's identity: the "gifts" they have received "and the calling of God are irrevocable." When I read "irrevocable" I am struck by the non-emotional and juridical nature of the word. It is similar to the proclamation of God's covenantal faithfulness. His reliability is celebrated throughout the sacred text. These declarations abound through the whole of Scripture: "God is just. God is righteous. He keeps His word. He is faithful to His covenant."

> *God is just. God is righteous. He keeps His word. He is faithful to His covenant.*

Thus, we similarly see, regarding Israel, that "... the gifts and the calling of God are irrevocable" (Romans 11:29). To "revoke" means to "end the validity or operation of a decree, decision, or promise."[50] When something is irrevocable, it is "unalterable,"[51] "not able to be changed, reversed, or recovered."[52]

Usually, "irrevocable" is used to describe a formal decision; official or personal. It is a word conveying contractual commitment. You can't cancel something that is irrevocable. You can't send it back and get your money refunded. I appreciate the work of practically every modern translator of Romans 11:29. They write, "the gifts and the calling of God are irrevocable." The non-revocable nature of God's gifts together with the Jewish people's irreversible calling is part of Paul's concluding argument.

Yet, it is not a precise translation! Rather, it is an unspoken corollary to what Paul was saying. It is true, but not exactly what Paul was trying to convey. What the apostle was teaching was much more personal than this. In fact, he used a word that conveys emotion, "*ametameleta.*"

The Greek word *ametameleta* means "without regret, without remorse."[53] We find the root of this word seven other times in the New Testament. To find out what Paul was conveying, let's look at these references. We discover the first two in Jesus' confrontation with religious leaders:

> "But what do you think? A man had two sons, and he came to the first and said, 'Son, go work today in the vineyard.' And he answered, 'I will not'; but afterward he regretted (*metamelomai*) it and went...For John came to you in the way of righteousness and you did not believe him; but the tax collectors and prostitutes did believe him; and you, seeing this, did not even feel remorse (*metamelomai*) afterward so as to believe him" (Matthew 21:28-29, 32).

Matthew also used this word to describe Judas Iscariot's emotional turmoil.

> Then when Judas, who had betrayed Him, saw that He had been condemned, he felt remorse

> (*metamelomai*) and returned the thirty pieces of silver to the chief priests and elders (Matthew 27:3).

In 2 Corinthians, there's a section where the root of this word is used twice and the exact word, once:

> For though I caused you sorrow by my letter, I do not regret (*metamelomai*) it; though I did regret (*metamelomai*) it—for I see that that letter caused you sorrow, though only for a while—I now rejoice, not that you were made sorrowful, but that you were made sorrowful to the point of repentance; for you were made sorrowful according to the will of God, so that you might not suffer loss in anything through us. For the sorrow that is according to the will of God produces a repentance without regret (*ametameleton*), leading to salvation, but the sorrow of the world produces death (2 Corinthians 7:8-10).

These verses show that there is an emotional component to this word. This is true of humanity, but is it true of God? Hebrews 7 has a description of God's determined, covenantal, steadfast emotional life:

> (For they indeed became priests without an oath, but He with an oath through the One who said to Him, "THE LORD HAS SWORN AND WILL NOT CHANGE HIS MIND (does not regret it - *metamelomai*), 'YOU ARE A PRIEST FOREVER'" (Hebrews 7:21b).

God established an eternal priesthood through the equivalent of a sacred oath. This quotation (Psalm 110:4) from the Septuagint employs the word used to describe Israel's irrevocable gifts and calling. He will not go back on His covenant. He will not repent of, or regret, His purposes.

The following three verses, in the Greek Septuagint (LXE), also use this word *ametameleta*:

> And Samuel did not see Saul again till the day of his death, for Samuel mourned after Saul, and the Lord repented (*metamelomai*) that he had made Saul king over Israel (1 Samuel 15:35, LXE).
>
> And God sent an angel to Jerusalem to destroy it: and as he was destroying, the Lord saw, and repented (*metamelomai*) for the evil, and said to the angel that was destroying, let it suffice thee; withhold thine hand. And the angel of the Lord stood by the threshing-floor of Orna the Jebusite (1 Chronicles 21:15, LXE).
>
> And he remembered his covenant, and repented (*metamelomai*) according to the multitude of his mercy (Psalm 106:45 LXE).

In using *ametameleta*, Paul was trying to convey this: in spite of everything, despite majority-Israel rejecting His Son and spurning His love, God is NOT SORRY that He gifted and called Israel. He is not sorry for the gifts He gave (Romans 9:4-5). He does not regret calling Israel. In this section, Paul was not revealing the judgments of God. He was opening up something about God's love for Israel. This word conveys emotion.

Here is a paraphrase that attempts to give the sense of the text:

> Concerning God's choosing Israel as a people: although they are enemies, they are still deeply loved for the sake of the Patriarchs.
>
> He does not sorrowfully regret the gifts He has given Israel or remorsefully wish He had never called them to Himself and His service. God has not rejected His people. (Heavily paraphrased Romans 11:28-29; 11:1, 2).

Do we believe that God delights in, and will eternally uphold, the Messiah's everlasting priesthood? If so, apply the same emotional sense to His relationship to Israel. Despite everything God has gone through in His relationship to Israel—the unfulfilled desire, jealousy, hurt, and anger—He does not regret lavishing His gifts upon them. Neither does God remorsefully repent of calling them. They are that valuable to Him. He loves the Jewish people and, because of the strength of that love, their gifts and calling are irrevocable.

God loves the Jewish people and, because of the strength of that love, their gifts and calling are irrevocable.

Putting 11:28-29 Together

Here are the verses we're looking at. Let's consider their context.

> From the standpoint of the gospel they are enemies for your sake, but from the standpoint of God's choice they are beloved for the sake of the fathers; for the gifts and the calling of God are irrevocable (Romans 11:28-29).

The context is this: Paul was contending with non-Jewish believers' perspectives of Israel. He warned the Gentiles about the potential for arrogance against the Jews. It is lamentably ironic that these warnings were rejected for practically two millennia, in most cases, down to this very day. While Paul was instructing them, warning them of that potential pitfall, he also revealed God's heart for the Church, the nations and both the remnant and majority of Israel. He wrote,

> *As far as the gospel is concerned, the bulk of the Jewish people are enemies for your sake.*

And finally, right here in those words, the culturally anti-Semitic believing Gentiles were gratified. I can caricature them as saying:

> *At last, finally something we agree with. That is a true statement which confirms and strengthens our perspective.*
>
> *They are enemies!*
>
> *Yes, I knew it!*

Then, suddenly, Paul reverses it and writes that the entire people, not just the remnant, are beloved, chosen, gifted, and called without remorse. Of necessity, this description includes majority-Israel who are trapped in unbelief. The apostle named them "enemies" just a few words earlier.

Despite the fact that they are "enemies" of the gospel, God does not regret calling them. Although He extends His hands in supplication to Israel to return, even while they reject His call, He does not regret choosing them.

Do you recall God's interaction with Samuel? The Lord said to the last of the Judges that He regretted calling Saul and had chosen another king (1 Samuel 15:35 LXE). Listen, Israel is not like Saul; the Jewish people are not rejected. God has not "regretted" calling the Jewish people. They are still called, chosen and beloved. We may ask, "Under what circumstances are they still called, chosen and beloved?" The answer to that question is, "Every, any, and all circumstances."

Are they called, chosen and beloved even while they are enemies and consequently hardened in their unbelieving perspective? Even though they are described as spiritually blind? "Yes," Paul wrote, "They are beloved." They are beloved and shall be preserved by God. Through the remnant's functioning like "salt" in the midst of the people, until the consummation of their calling, Israel shall be sustained by their Creator.

> Thus says the LORD, Who gives the sun for light by day and the fixed order of the moon and the stars for light by night, Who stirs up the sea so that its waves roar; the LORD of hosts is His name: If this fixed order departs from before Me, declares the LORD, then the offspring of Israel also will cease from being a nation before Me forever. Thus says the LORD, If the heavens above can be measured and the foundations of the earth searched out below, then I will also cast off all the offspring of Israel for all that they have done, declares the LORD (Jeremiah 31:35-37).

When all Israel returns to God, what is written shall come to pass. It shall be "life from the dead." This is the foreordained destiny of God's beloved people. And why are they beloved, after all they are "enemies?" Paul stressed that Israel is especially loved because of the love God has for the Patriarchs.

Paul stressed that Israel is especially loved because of the love God has for the Patriarchs.

God's Mercy: An Emotion

One aspect of God's mercy that is not often celebrated is mercy's origin. Ephesians 2:4 clearly states that God has mercy because of His great love. Consider that when you read the introduction to Paul's conclusion of this matter.

> For just as you once were disobedient to God, but now have been shown mercy because of their disobedience, so these also now have been disobedient, that because of the mercy shown to you they also may now be shown mercy. For God has shut up all in disobedience so that He may show mercy to all (Romans 11:30-32).

His mercy proceeds from His love. In this case, His love for Israel and the nations. His mercy will not be thwarted. God's purposes will be accomplished.

Summation

What emotions towards Israel are displayed in Romans 9-11? What emotions are provoked in God because of Israel?

Let's dare to personalize the revelation Paul shared with the Roman believers. Through all Paul wrote, we can hear God say:

> *My people, I chose you. I choose you. I call and adorn you. I love you to this day.*
>
> *Israel, to Me, you are so valuable that, no matter what, I preserve you and I will restore you.*
>
> *I plead with you to respond, but you refuse to return. I do not leave you unpunished; neither do I force you to respond to Me. You have rejected Me and that has severe consequences; but I will never ultimately reject you. You are My people.*
>
> *You were called to reach the nations, but I could not reach you. So, I turn to them. I am not waiting for you any longer; the time for reconciling the nations is now!*
>
> *I exalt them and bring them in to participate in the life, which is your life, and into a calling, which is your calling. I love them and dignify them with your calling to make you jealous and provoke you to return to Me.*
>
> *You may be hostile to the message of My heart, but I am not hostile towards you. Despite your rejecting My love, despite your refusal to return, I do not regret revealing My affections for you and to you. I do not*

regret lavishing My gifts upon you and I am not sorry I chose you.

Although you do not return, when the time is right, I shall return to you. I shall come from heaven's Zion and restore you. I love your fathers so much that, for their sake, I have a special love for you.

From the very beginning, I loved Jacob and I shall come and remove iniquity from My beloved.

When you are restored I shall treat you with great honor. Because I love you, your calling and gifts will be realized in a greater way than you could imagine. Here is your destiny: you are the means through which I shall release the Kingdom's fullness. I have not forgotten your calling. I have reserved this privilege for you.

The nations I have redeemed will rejoice in your return. They shall marvel at what I do through you. Joining you, they shall celebrate My mercy. You shall lead the praise, for a full revelation of My love, mercy, and glory will be yours and I will be glorified in you.

10

For the Sake of the Patriarchs

IN THE APOSTOLIC PROCLAMATION, IN THE MESSIAH'S apologetic for the resurrection, and in the book of Hebrews, our God is known as the God of Abraham, Isaac and Jacob. That is who He is today, and right now, as you read this, that God has a unique love for the Jewish people. They are "...beloved for the sake of the fathers" (Romans 11:28b).

What a curious thought. Where did Paul get this? What is its biblical background? As you read this chapter, you will begin to uncover the nature of the love that stirs God's heart for Israel. We will examine some background and a poorly translated Hebrew word: *chashaq.*

Chashaq

Chashaq is an interesting Hebrew word. It connotes desire, longing, attraction, and consequent attachment. In the context of relationships, *chashaq* is used to describe a common experience and not a particularly pristine one, at that. Here are two verses where it is used to express a common aspect of human experience:

> But Hamor spoke with them, saying, "The soul of my son Shechem longs for your daughter; please give her to him in marriage" (Genesis 34:8).
>
> ...and see among the captives a beautiful woman, and have a desire for her and would take her as a wife for yourself (Deuteronomy 21:11).

In these two verses, *chashaq* is translated 'longs for' and 'desire.' The context is plain. The meaning is clear. It describes the emotion a man has when he is strongly attracted to a woman, finding her so attractive that he wants to marry (be attached to) her.

In Psalm 91:14 this word is used to describe a relationship from man to God. It is translated 'loved' in the New American Standard:

> Because he has loved (*chashaq*) Me, therefore I will deliver him; I will set him securely on high, because he has known My name.

Here are some other translations of Psalm 91a:

> ESV: Because he holds fast to me in love...

> Tanak: Because he is devoted to Me...

> Young's Literal Translation: Because in Me he hath delighted...

Chashaq speaks of love, desire and attraction that produces attachment. This word is also utilized to describe the love God has for Israel and the patriarchs.

A Common Misunderstanding

Surprisingly, this word is found in one of the primary verses mistakenly used to promote a distorted perspective of biblical love. Many believe that God's love is not a feeling provoked by the beloved. They contend that holy love is an act of the "lover's" will. This outlook cripples our capacity to appreciate the reality of God's love for the Jewish people. *Chashaq* is found in Deuteronomy 7:7 and is often mistranslated "set His love on you":[54]

> "The LORD did not set His love on you nor choose you because you were more in number than any

> of the peoples, for you were the fewest of all peoples"

When the words "set His love on you" are read, quoted, or taught, they are often interpreted as pointing to God's willpower. These words seem to indicate that 'His love' was utilized through choice. Apparently, God picked up His love and, through the use of volition, placed (set) His love upon Israel. This view maintains that God chooses to love, and that this love is free from any loveliness found in the beloved. This opinion is often expressed by those who stress a specific view of God's sovereignty. In fact, the Bible teaches that love chooses, but love is not mere choice. One chooses how to express love, but love is the motive, not the result, of choice. The strength of the love determines the nature of the choice. (I've written at length about this in *God's True Love.*)

Deuteronomy 7:7 is part of a sentence and, thus, it is not a complete thought. Many tend to utilize this fragment to stress (often hyperbolically) that there was absolutely nothing worthwhile about Israel that warranted God's choice. They reason that He loved the unlovely through unadulterated volition for His own glory, and that the qualities of the beloved had nothing to do with this love. Therefore, people actually believe that this is what divine love is like. However, the sentence does not end at the finish of verse 7. It continues. Here is the entire sentence:

> "The LORD did not set His love on you nor choose you because you were more in number than any of the peoples, for you were the fewest of all peoples, but because the LORD loved you and kept the oath which He swore to your forefathers, the LORD brought you out by a mighty hand and redeemed you from the house of slavery, from the hand of Pharaoh king of Egypt" (Deuteronomy 7:7, 8).

What these verses communicate is that the LORD delivered Israel because He loved them. He was attracted to them; He found them to be lovely. The number of worshipers, something which might attract a lesser god's attention, did not figure into God's equation. It did not count as a factor in the LORD's heart being drawn to Israel. Additionally, He kept the oath He swore to the patriarchs. In these verses, it is revealed that the God of Israel did not choose them so He might display His splendor. He chose Israel because He loved them and was faithful to their fathers.

In these verses, it is revealed that the God of Israel did not choose them so He might display His splendor. He chose Israel because He loved them and was faithful to their fathers.

As in our earlier examples, the Hebrew word in Deuteronomy 7:7 translated "set his love upon" is *chashaq*. We have seen that this doesn't imply volition. The word connotes 'attraction and attachment' that is so strong that the lover, acting upon that emotion, chooses them to be his beloved.[55] *Chashaq* also describes the same type of love the LORD had for the patriarchs. In Deuteronomy 10:15, it is also mistranslated: 'set His affection.'

> "Yet on your fathers did the LORD set His affection (*chashaq*) to love them, and He chose their descendants after them, even you above all peoples, as it is this day" (Deuteronomy 10:15).

The God who identifies Himself by the names of the Patriarchs, the God of Abraham, Isaac and Jacob, loved those men. He found something in them that attracted Him to them. He found delight in them. He loved them to the degree that He entered into covenant with them. He loved. He chose. What attracted God's love is not mentioned in verse seven. An aspect of this attraction is hinted at in verse eight when the covenant vows made to the patriarchs are brought to mind. First read the common mistranslation from the King James Version:

> "The LORD did not set His love on you nor choose you because you were more in number than any of the peoples, for you were the fewest of all peoples, but because the LORD loved you and kept the oath which He swore to your forefathers..." (Deuteronomy 7:7-8a)

Now examine how different Deuteronomy 7:7-8a looks when *chashaq* is translated according to its relational intention. I took the liberty to place the actual definition of *chashaq* into the text. Please read it.

> The LORD (was not attracted to you, did not desire you), or choose you, because you were more in number than any of the peoples, for you were the fewest of all peoples, but because the LORD loved you and kept the oath which He swore to your forefathers...

Doesn't it feel different than "did not set His love on you"? Deuteronomy 7:7-8 is intended to teach that God was radically attracted to Israel and the Jewish people, that He chose them because He really loved them, and, also, was faithful to the oath He swore to the patriarchs. This passage teaches that God chose Israel because of God's strong loving attraction to them. His choice was not based upon His incredible volition. Yet, Deuteronomy 7:7 is often taught as if the verse said this:

> *The LORD did not find anything attractive about you so as to provoke Him to choose you. After all, there were not a lot of you, in fact you were the fewest of all peoples.*

> *However, He exercised His sovereign choice, to show how worthy of glory He is. His choice of you unworthy people proves that all His actions proceed from unmerited favor.*

If it were a matter of making a decision for His glory's sake, like an insecure narcissist, He would not have chosen such a weak, insignificant group. After all, Proverbs 14:28a states, "In a multitude of people is a king's glory" (Proverbs 14:28a).

God's Motive: Holy Love

Let's continue to contrast the way people teach about God "setting His love on" Israel with what the Bible actually says. A friend applied the same logic used in translating and preaching Deuteronomy 7:7 to how the word is used in Deuteronomy 21:11, which reads:

> ...and see among the captives a beautiful woman, and have a desire (*chashaq*) for her and would take her as a wife for yourself (Deuteronomy 21:11).

If we force *chashaq* to conform to the theological necessities of certain doctrinal systems, perhaps it would read this way:

> *If you see among the captives a woman that does not appeal to you (and sort of repels you), and if you have no desire (chashaq) for her, but really want to reveal how wonderful you are by taking her as a wife for yourself...*[56]

Yet, the reason God desired the descendants of the patriarchs was because He loved them! One might argue, "But the Bible says they were the fewest of all peoples." Nevertheless, He saw them as lovely. Therefore, He chose them. He wanted them as a man desires a woman he finds to be lovely. Here is some confirmation found in a respected commentary on Deuteronomy:

> The Lord set his love on you... The verb means "desire" or "want." The Septuagint translates with a verb that means "prefer," "choose." And chose you: this additional verbal phrase may be joined to the previous one, as follows: "he decided you were the people he wanted, and so he chose you," and the whole verse may be restructured as follows:
>
> The Lord [or, Yahweh] decided that you were the people he wanted, and chose you.[57]

Remember, God does not find "glorious" what humanity sees as "glorious." Matthew 16:23 is a reminder of this principle:

> But He turned and said to Peter, "Get behind Me, Satan! You are a stumbling block to Me; for you are not setting your mind on God's interests, but man's" (Matthew 16:23).

For those who forget about God's priorities, remember that He is not attracted to human wisdom, power and wealth.

> Thus says the LORD, "Let not a wise man boast of his wisdom, and let not the mighty man boast of his might, let not a rich man boast of his riches; but let him who boasts boast of this, that he understands and knows Me, that I am the LORD who exercises lovingkindness, justice and righteousness on earth; for I delight in these things," declares the LORD (Jeremiah 9:23-24).

For the Sake of the Patriarchs: Transgenerational Love

Not only did He love Israel, not only was He attracted and attached to them, but they were also loved because God loved their ancestors. The One who chose Israel gave promises to the patriarchs concerning their descendants. This is a foundational promise made to Abraham:

The One who chose Israel gave promises to the patriarchs concerning their descendants.

> God said, "No, but Sarah your wife will bear you a son, and you shall call his name Isaac; and I will establish My covenant with him for an everlasting covenant for his descendants after him" (Genesis 17:19).

God confirmed His promise to Isaac:

> The LORD appeared to [Isaac] the same night and said, "I am the God of your father Abraham; do not fear, for I am with you. I will bless you, and multiply your descendants, for the sake of My servant Abraham" (Genesis 26:24).

Isaac's unlikely heir, Jacob, heard the same word:

> And behold, the LORD stood above it and said [to Jacob], "I am the LORD, the God of your father Abraham and the God of Isaac; the land on which you lie, I will give it to you and to your descendants" (Genesis 28:13).

And Joseph revealed the way the patriarchs viewed themselves.

> Joseph said to his brothers, "I am about to die, but God will surely take care of you and bring you up from this land to the land which He promised on oath to Abraham, to Isaac and to Jacob" (Genesis 50:24).

This understanding is reinforced in the New Testament. Paul wrote:

> ...they are beloved for the sake of the fathers (Romans 11:28b).

God's love for Israel is not just the testimony of the Old Testament. It is a relevant part of biblical faith. The revelation of this reality is intended to help shape the heart and hope of the Church. That is why Paul spelled it out.

Transgenerational Covenant Between Friends

God's love for the Jewish people is similar to Jonathan and David's covenant.

> Then Jonathan made a covenant with David because he loved him as himself (1 Samuel 18:3).

The covenant between these battle-hardened warriors had its origin in a deep love. It was proclaimed as valid from generation to generation

> Jonathan said to David, "Go in safety, inasmuch as we have sworn to each other in the name of the LORD, saying, 'The LORD will be between me and you, and between my descendants and your descendants forever'" (1 Samuel 20:42a).

Love was the impetus that called forth the covenant. In this love-covenant, David swore that he would care for Jonathan's descendants. His concern for those descendants illustrates and follows the pattern of God's attachment to Israel. The LORD loved Israel and also confirmed the oath that He had sworn to the patriarchs. They were the descendants of Abraham, the man who loved God and was His friend:

David swore that he would care for Jonathan's descendants. His concern for those descendants illustrates and follows the pattern of God's attachment to Israel.

> Did You not, O our God, drive out the inhabitants of this land before Your people Israel and give it to the descendants of Abraham Your friend forever? (2 Chronicles 20:7)

> But you, Israel, My servant, Jacob whom I have chosen, descendant of Abraham My friend... (Isaiah 41:8)

In these two verses, we find a key as to why God made an oath to Abraham. God's motive was His delight in the patriarch's love of God. Astonishingly, the emphasis in these verses is not on God's love for Abraham, but Abraham's love for God! He was the man who was God's friend. Abraham loved God enough to be His friend. Think of this: a man befriends God ... and it affects the way God feels about that man. God says, "He is My friend." It brings to mind Psalm 91:14:

> Because he has loved (*chashaq*) Me, therefore I will...

I wish it were not so, but love for God is a rare thing. Friendship towards God is precious to God. It moves God to a love which is so faithful that, according to Paul, it can endure through the ages and withstand any lack of reciprocity. Like the psalmist, as with Abraham, the Lord has constructed our relationship with Him so as to be mutual.

> Therefore it says, "Draw near to God and He will draw near to you" (James 4:8a).

This Revelation is Relevant

We looked at Deuteronomy 7:7-8. What we found is an attraction and a transgenerational covenant of loyalty born of love. It is the same principle found in Deuteronomy 4:37-38:

> Because He loved your fathers, therefore He chose their descendants after them. And He personally brought you from Egypt by His great power, driving out from before you nations greater and mightier than you, to bring you in and to give you their land for an inheritance, as it is today (Deuteronomy 4:37-38).

God has not outgrown this love. This is the love that God has for all of Israel today. The New Testament puts it this way:

> ...as regards election, they are beloved for the sake of their forefathers (Romans 11:28b).

They are chosen and beloved in the same way and for the same reason: God loved and chose their ancestors. Dare we believe it remains the same type of love? Can we dare to disbelieve? Read this again.

> ...as regards election, they are beloved for the sake of their forefathers (Romans 11:28b).

Today, they are loved for the sake of the patriarchs. God has not changed. The nature of His love remains the same. The enduring strength of His attraction undergirds the power of His choice. He is attached to them. He longs for all Israel to return to Him. God is looking for those who, like Abraham, are His friends and are willing to enter into fellowship with His heart. You are called to be that type of friend. Will you love those He loves because you love Him?

Summary

Here is what we found when we studied the ways *chashaq* is used in the Bible to describe relationships. Twice it is used to speak of the attraction of a man towards a woman he finds to be beautiful. We have seen two clear examples of it being used to inform the reader of God's attraction to people: once to Israel and once to the patriarchs. Once it is used to portray the love the psalmist had for God which provoked a response in God towards the lover. We examined Deuteronomy 7:7, a verse popularly used to promote the view that God's love has nothing to do with attraction, although it is infused with vocabulary that teaches the opposite: God saw, God delighted in, and God gives Himself to the objects of His love.

This is what Paul said God's love is like. It is a strong, enduring attachment that has its roots in an ancient relationship the Creator had with the Patriarchs. Although it is not often emphasized, this love is alive. God is not the God of the dead, but of the living. The Patriarchs are alive. God's love for their children is alive.

Pray:

Those who have gratefully received the forgiveness and new life offered in the Messiah have a unique personal relationship with God. We expect Him to be concerned about every aspect of our lives. Jesus said that every hair on our heads is numbered. God is concerned about us.

Let's reciprocate.

He loves the Jewish people for the sake of the Patriarchs. Ask Him if he would favor you with increased fellowship with this aspect of His affections.

11

God's Anguish

O God! That You would get Your people back!

PAUL WROTE OF HIS ANGUISH CONCERNING HIS brethren.

> I am speaking the truth in Christ—I am not lying; my conscience bears me witness in the Holy Spirit—that I have great sorrow and unceasing anguish in my heart. For I could wish that I myself were accursed and cut off from Christ for the sake of my brothers, my kinsmen according to the flesh (Romans 9:1-3).

The apostle's grief mirrored God's.

Israel's prophets revealed the mystery of God's heartbreak over His people. It is not a comfortable topic and is not easily accessed by the faint of heart. Let's look at it, anyway.

Heartbreak

> ...how I have been broken... (Ezekiel 6:9b)

Ezekiel had overwhelming visions of God's glory. He saw, heard and experienced God and His throne. His perception of the appearance of God's splendor (Ezekiel 1:28) was complemented by the revelations he received of God's heart. I do not know which provokes more wonder.

I find Ezekiel 6:9 to be particularly painful. It relates the reality of God's heartbreak over Israel. This verse is worth studying.

> Then those of you who escape will remember Me among the nations to which they will be carried captive, how I have been hurt [broken in pieces], by their adulterous hearts which turned away from Me, and by their eyes which played the harlot after their idols; and they will loathe themselves in their own sight for the evils which they have committed, for all their abominations (Ezekiel 6:9).

Most of us can empathize with heartbroken people. But are we called to empathize with God? Yes, we are. And we can. The context of Ezekiel 6:9 is a judgment oracle. God commissioned the prophet to release a verdict of imminent wrath. God was going to smash the places where His people committed spiritual adultery. Idolatrous shrines were going to be destroyed. The incense altars would be smashed (6:4) together with the idols (6:6). The prophesied destruction, carnage and diaspora (scattering) are terrifying.

Are we called to empathize with God? Yes, we are. And we can.

> Your altars shall become desolate, and your incense altars shall be broken (smashed), and I will cast down your slain before your idols. And I will lay the dead bodies of the people of Israel before their idols, and I will scatter your bones around your altars. Wherever you dwell, the cities shall be waste and the high places ruined, so that your altars will be waste and ruined, your idols broken and destroyed, your incense altars cut down, and your works wiped out (Ezekiel 6:4-6).

God charged Israel to destroy Canaan's idols. Yet, centuries later, we find Israel prostrate before pagan shrines. In Ezekiel 6 the LORD said He would destroy this disgusting idolatry. The word the prophet used to describe

God's attitude towards His rivals was derisive. He contemptuously referred to these idols as piles of sculpted excrement, "*gillulim.*" Ezekiel's favorite word for idols is *gillulim*, which means "dung pellets." The term is first used in chapter 6 where it appears five times (vs. 4, 5, 6, 9, 13) ...[58]

One lexicon described these idols as "logs, blocks, shapeless things...doll-images, dungy things."[59] God commanded Israel to root out the Canaanites from the Land due to their wickedness.[60] Yet, now the LORD was going to uproot Israel. He would accomplish Israel's dread commission to cleanse the land, but the object of wrath would be His own people. This is my interpretation of what the prophet reported:

> *Thus says the LORD, "See what I'm going to do to the incense altars. I'm going to break them. I'm going to smash them!*
>
> *"Do you see the idols before which you burned incense? I'm going to crush those vile, worthless things...*
>
> *"Why?*
>
> *"Israel, this is what you have done to My heart! You've broken My heart."*

Ezekiel 6 prophesied that the LORD would smash Israel's idolatry in the same way His heart was broken by His people.

> How I have been broken over their whoring heart that has departed from me and over their eyes that go whoring after their idols (Ezekiel 6:9b).

The word (*shavar*) used to describe God's emotions means "to break, rupture" the heart.[61] Someone thus afflicted is filled with distress.[62] One lexicon gives this sense of the word: to break any one's mind, i.e. to affect with sadness.[63] Israel's unfaithfulness really did affect God's heart. This is not a mere anthropomorphism. This was not a game. The emotions God experienced were real. J. E. Smith wrote the following concerning Ezekiel 6:

> "Their 'adulterous hearts' and wandering eyes had brought pain to the heart of God."[64]

When referring to the emotions, the word translated "broken" conveys intense suffering. Sorrow over sin, which leads to repentance, is an emotion akin to the slaughtering of a sacrifice. It is like an emotional bloodletting in the presence of holiness.

> The sacrifices of God are a broken (*shavar*) spirit;
> a broken (*shavar*) and contrite heart, O God, you
> will not despise (Psalm 51:17).

When it describes the condition of the human spirit (Psalm 51:17) it is evidenced by "wailing" (Isaiah 65:14).

> Behold, My servants will shout joyfully with a glad heart, but you will cry out with a heavy heart, and you will wail with a broken (*shavar*) spirit (Isaiah 65:14).

What the prophet opens up to us is a view of the brokenhearted outrage of Israel's covenant Partner. This does not describe a judicious, cold upholding of an external principle. Let us pay attention. This is the revelatory word the LORD gave to His confidante, the prophet, who dared report it to us. The NET Bible's notes add,

> The image of God being "broken" is startling, but perfectly natural within the metaphorical framework of God as offended husband. The idiom must refer to the intense grief that Israel's unfaithfulness caused God.[65]

We can relate to this type of experience. But what must it take for the Omnipotent One to experience heartbreak? What type of love is strong enough to break the heart of God? The Messiah's heartbreak is prophetically described in Psalm 69. This psalm was often quoted by the authors of the New Testament. In it they found descriptions of Jesus' zeal for the Father's house, of the Messiah's sufferings, and of prophesied imprecations upon the gospel's adversaries. Here are the well-known verses concerning Calvary:

> Reproaches (insults, disgrace) have broken (*shavar*) my heart, so that I am in despair. I looked for pity, but there was none, and for comforters, but I found none. They gave me poison for food, and for my thirst they gave me sour wine to drink (Psalm 69:20-21).

This word (*shavar*) is used over 200 times in the Hebrew Scriptures. It is only used once to directly describe God. His strength was not broken. His omniscience was not ruptured. It was His heart. His heart was broken. What do we find when we focus on this foreshadowing of the crucifixion in Psalm 69? Jesus' experience on the cross is the only other time this word may be used to describe God's heart. Israel's rejection broke His heart.[66]

This God draws near to, and heals, those whose hearts are broken (*shavar*).

> The LORD is near to the brokenhearted (*shavar*) and saves the crushed in spirit (Psalm 34:18).

Psalm 147:3 confirms this:

> He heals the brokenhearted (*shavar*) and binds up their wounds (Psalm 147:3).

But what is the remedy for the LORD? Who can heal His heart?

Jeremiah, Jesus and God's Broken Heart

It may help us see God's anguish by examining an often-overlooked aspect of the Messiah's ministry. The Messiah was the physical manifestation of the invisible God. How did Jesus' contemporaries see Him?

> Now when Jesus came into the district of Caesarea Philippi, He was asking His disciples, "Who do people say that the Son of Man is?" And they said, "Some say John the Baptist; and others, Elijah; but still others, Jeremiah, or one of the prophets" (Matthew 16:13-14).

John baptized and preached repentance. Jesus preached and baptized, too. Elijah worked miracles and called Israel back to God. Jesus did miracles and preached the good news of the Kingdom. Yeshua was the supreme prophet of Israel. The holy aspects of each prophetic ministry are summed up in Him. Any of the prophets could have been the basis of comparison, but Jeremiah is mentioned. What did Jeremiah and Jesus have in common? Here is a brief list of how the analogy is fitting:

1. Jeremiah prophesied a New Covenant. Jesus inaugurated it.

2. Jeremiah was rejected, ridiculed, and persecuted; so was Jesus.

3. Jeremiah proclaimed judgment: the destruction of Jerusalem and the Temple. Jesus did, too.

4. Jeremiah wept. Jeremiah suffered over the Jewish people. He foretold the Babylonian Diaspora. Jeremiah agonized, he prophesied restoration. Jesus did, also.

Here are two verses which describe the inner life of Jeremiah, the herald of the first Diaspora. First look at Jeremiah 4:19:

> My soul, my soul! I am in anguish! Oh, my heart! My heart is pounding in me; I cannot be silent, because you have heard, O my soul, the sound of the trumpet, the alarm of war (Jeremiah 4:19).

Now, consider the Jeremiah-Jesus connection in Jeremiah 9:1.

> Oh that my head were waters and my eyes a fountain of tears, that I might weep day and night for the slain of the daughter of my people! (Jeremiah 9:1)

Like Jeremiah, Jesus was despised, a man of sorrows as described in Isaiah 53:3.

> He was despised and forsaken of men, a man of sorrows and acquainted with grief; and like one from whom men hide their face He was despised, and we did not esteem Him (Isaiah 53:3).

Like Jeremiah, Jesus convulsively wept over Jerusalem's coming catastrophic judgment:

> When He approached Jerusalem, He saw the city and wept over it, saying, "If you had known in this day, even you, the things which make for peace! But now they have been hidden from your eyes. For the days will come upon you when your enemies will throw up a barricade against you, and surround you and hem you in on every side, and they will level you to the ground and your children within you, and they will not leave in you one stone upon another, because you did not recognize the time of your visitation" (Luke 19:41-44).

Like Jeremiah, Jesus prophesied judgment, merciless slaughter, destruction, the Diaspora, and coming restoration.

> But when you see Jerusalem surrounded by armies, then recognize that her desolation is near. Then those who are in Judea must flee to the mountains, and those who are in the midst of the city must leave, and those who are in the country must not enter the city; because these are days of vengeance, so that all things which are written will be fulfilled.
>
> Woe to those who are pregnant and to those who are nursing babies in those days; for there will be great distress upon the land and wrath to this people; and they will fall by the edge of the sword, and will be led captive into all the nations; and Jerusalem will be trampled underfoot by the Gentiles until the times of the Gentiles are fulfilled (Luke 21:20-24).

Here is another prophecy from the Messiah in Luke 23:26-31:

> When they led Him away, they seized a man, Simon of Cyrene, coming in from the country, and placed on him the cross to carry behind Jesus. And following Him was a large crowd of the people, and of women who were mourning and lamenting Him. But Jesus turning to them said, "Daughters of Jerusalem, stop weeping for Me, but weep for yourselves and for your children. For behold, the days are coming when they will say, 'Blessed are the barren, and the wombs that never bore, and the breasts that never nursed.' Then they will begin TO SAY TO THE MOUNTAINS, 'FALL ON US,' AND TO THE HILLS, 'COVER US.' For if they do these things when the tree is green, what will happen when it is dry?" (Luke 23:26-31)

Picture Jesus betrayed, forsaken, beaten and condemned. He is walking to Golgotha. Look! He is still prophesying. In Luke's account, this brokenhearted oracle was the last thing He said before He was crucified. Luke's account continued, quoting Jesus from the Cross.

> Two others also, who were criminals, were being led away to be put to death with Him. When they came to the place called The Skull, there they crucified Him and the criminals, one on the right and the other on the left. But Jesus was saying, "Father, forgive them; for they do not know what they are doing." And they cast lots, dividing up His garments among themselves (Luke 23:32-34).

First, He prophesied to the "daughters of Jerusalem" (23:26-31), and then (23:32-34) He offered up His life and interceded for Israel. It is as if the Messiah could not get His people's impending tribulation out of His heart. Despite the coming wrath, He sought to ameliorate the coming judgment because they did not recognize the time of their visitation. Read His intercession in the light of His prophecy.

His prophecy:

> "For behold, the days are coming when they will say, 'Blessed are the barren, and the wombs that never bore, and the breasts that never nursed.' Then they will begin TO SAY TO THE MOUNTAINS, 'FALL ON US,' AND TO THE HILLS, 'COVER US'" (Luke 23:29-30).

His intercession:

> But Jesus was saying, "Father, forgive them; for they do not know what they are doing" (Luke 23:34a).

What does this say about God's heart for Israel? God's heart, incarnate in the Messiah, reflexively called out for His people's pardon. A day is coming when this intercession will be answered to the uttermost. Israel will be forgiven, restored, and be an unmitigated blessing amongst the nations.

Peter's Preaching

Jesus prophesied judgment upon Jerusalem, Israel's coming Diaspora, and His people's future restoration. His disciples took note. They rehearsed His words as they meditated upon the last week before His crucifixion. Imagine the power of Jesus' prophecies on the emotional life of the primitive Messianic Community. I think we can see that influence in Peter's proclamation on Pentecost. As you read his message's conclusion, keep in mind that Peter was convinced that apart from unforeseen national repentance, Jerusalem and the Temple were going to be destroyed. Peter was contending for the life of his people in the face of impending doom:

> "Therefore let all the house of Israel know for certain that God has made Him both Lord and Christ—this Jesus whom you crucified." And with many other words he solemnly testified and kept on exhorting them, saying, "Be saved from this perverse generation!" (Acts 2:36, 40)

The apostle was aware of Israel's transgression in the light of Jesus' intercession. Look how he pleaded with his people:

> But you disowned the Holy and Righteous One and asked for a murderer to be granted to you, but put to death the Prince of life, the one whom God raised from the dead, a fact to which we are witnesses. And now, brethren, I know that you

> acted in ignorance, just as your rulers did also (Acts 3:14-15, 17).

His proclamation was one of heartache and hope, accountability and amnesty. With eyes opened to the gathering storm, Peter boldly pronounced the potential realization of the prophetic promises to Israel. Perhaps he hoped that if Israel repented, the coming destruction would be averted by the Lord's return.

> But the things which God announced beforehand by the mouth of all the prophets, that His Christ would suffer, He has thus fulfilled. Therefore, repent and return, so that your sins may be wiped away, in order that times of refreshing may come from the presence of the Lord; and that He may send Jesus, the Christ appointed for you, whom heaven must receive until the period of restoration of all things about which God spoke by the mouth of His holy prophets from ancient time (Acts 3:18-21).

Do we believe that the Messiah, like Jeremiah, foretold Jerusalem's destruction? Do we believe He prophesied the dispersion of His people? Did His apostles believe Him and pay attention to what He said? Undoubtedly, and we can conclude that this expectation was integrated into the faith-structure of these disciples. If they really believed this, we can be assured that this conviction helped shape their culture. Therefore, in the midst of joy, due to the Messiah's resurrection and the presence of the Spirit, the Apostolic Community was also filled with apprehension. Their dread of the coming Diaspora should be considered when we read the report of their warnings and their writings.

The content of the apostolic proclamation to Israel is typified in Peter's preaching. He was the paradigmatic Apostle to Israel. To read inspired records of his messages

Even after His ascension, Jesus was reaching out to His people through messengers who carried His heart and conveyed the Holy Spirit's desire to rescue Israel.

without discerning Peter's emotions does him and his words a disservice. Such a reading distorts the intent of the Spirit who anointed the apostle. This man's ministry was a revelation of God's burning heart for the Jewish people. Even after His ascension, Jesus was reaching out to His people through messengers who carried His heart and conveyed the Holy Spirit's desire to rescue Israel. The Spirit's burden for Israel can be seen in the Messiah's lament as He pilgrimaged one last time to Jerusalem.

> O Jerusalem, Jerusalem, the city that kills the prophets and stones those sent to her! How often I wanted to gather your children together, just as a hen gathers her brood under her wings, and you would not have it! (Luke 13:34)

The apostles had been discipled by Jesus. After Pentecost, they had His Spirit dwelling in them. The Spirit strengthened their attitudes towards the Jewish people which had been formed through interaction with Jesus. They had learned firsthand from the Messiah. His Holy Spirit reinforced what they had received. Their love for their people was a supernaturally enhanced devotion. God's love empowered their love.

To sum up:

Ezekiel proclaimed God's heartbroken love for Israel. To this day his message is shocking. The prophet was specially molded so the LORD might speak that startling word. It took a broken-hearted widower to speak for a heartbroken God.

Jeremiah's grief-stricken love was spiritually enhanced. It was holy. The emotions he endured were prophetic. They represented the God who had set him apart. Sometimes, when one reads his oracles, it is hard to tell whether the laments are the anguished articulation of the prophet or his God. Jeremiah's tears revealed God's heart. The ancient records of those cries reveal some mysteries of the LORD's emotions.

Some, observing Jesus, thought He resembled Jeremiah. We noted the Messiah's grief and the similarity between His and Jeremiah's prophetic burden. Jeremiah wept and prophesied destruction; so did Jesus. Jesus' demonstrations of compassion and grief reveal the Father's innermost emotions towards Israel.

Peter urged his countrymen to repent and be saved from the foretold wrath. His heart was stirred for those who would join the remnant of Israel. Despite the prophesied devastation, he proclaimed the promise of the coming Kingdom. Peter longed to see his people come into the promises prophesied over preceding centuries.

Ezekiel's revelation of God's brokenness complemented Jeremiah's prophecies. These oracles revealed God's grieving heart through emotion, act, and word. Jesus incarnated God's torn heart for His people. Peter fought for his people's salvation. His message mirrored the Messiah's cry for mercy. His preaching preserved the hope that perhaps it was not too late to avert the full extent of the coming judgment. This apostle's preaching and motive manifested God's pursuing love.

It is wise to recall that Ezekiel, Jeremiah, the Lord Jesus and Peter spoke of more than God's heartbreak and judgment. They also proclaimed and, at times, prophetically demonstrated, the promise of Israel's future restored relationship to God. They spoke of the glorious things that would follow that transition. The pattern of the gospel (God pursuing humanity and reconciling fallen people to Himself) is portrayed in the drama of the God of Israel's relationship to His people. This is the same God. He unchangingly loves Israel. Remember, Jesus is the same today as He was then, and He will be the same tomorrow. Yeshua shall always carry and convey the God of Abraham, Isaac and Jacob's impassioned love for the Jewish people.

Yeshua shall always carry and convey the God of Abraham, Isaac and Jacob's impassioned love for the Jewish people.

This type of love can hurt, grieve, warn, and motivate labor for Israel's restoration. It can generate intense emotional turmoil. It is deep love that can produce such pressure as to ultimately erupt and break open the heart which contains it. Paul experienced this.

> I am speaking the truth in Christ – I am not lying; my conscience bears me witness in the Holy Spirit—that I have great sorrow and unceasing anguish in my heart. For I could wish that I myself were accursed and cut off from Christ for the sake of my brothers, my kinsmen according to the flesh (Romans 9:1-3).

Paul's anguish mirrored the broken heart of his God. As we get to know God as He really is, and understand His emotions concerning the Jewish people, our hearts may get broken, too. An intercessors' first priority is to identify with God's heart. When you receive this revelation, it may be a burden too hard to bear. For His sake, it might break your heart, too.

If so, you're in good company.

12

Their Own Olive Tree

UPON OCCASION, I RUN INTO STATEMENTS SO culturally foreign that I do a double take. Here's one.

> I, Paul, am writing this with my own hand, I will repay it (not to mention to you that you owe to me even your own self as well) (Philemon 1:19).

Paul asked Philemon to do him a "favor." This request was not made through private correspondence. It was read in a house church setting. It is read to this day. Paul publicly pressured him. Can you imagine this? I never heard any preacher say, "You owe to me even your own self because I brought the gospel to you." Obviously, Paul was not shy and the culture in which the New Testament was written took things like honor, patronage, and debt seriously. Philemon was a recipient of spiritual patronage. If he rejected Paul's request, he would dishonor his spiritual patron. Also, for Philemon to disregard Paul's request would be seen as disgraceful. In this culture, one abhorred unresolved social debt, and this man owed Paul.

In Romans, a similar cultural phenomenon took place. Newly converted Gentile Romans and the Messianic Jewish Romans were called to love one another, fellowship with one another, receive one another, and give each other the benefit of one another's spiritual gifts. Paul worked with a metaphor to make plain their vital, organic, mutual fellowship. The metaphor is "the Olive Tree." This metaphor follows on the heels of Paul dishing out ample

The gospel of salvation Paul preached was predicated on humility.

helpings of humble pie. The gospel of salvation Paul preached was predicated on humility.

- Recognize that there is a glorious and powerful Creator.
- Recognize that you are a Gentile sinner.
- Recognize that you are a Jewish sinner.
- Recognize that there is no difference in God's sight between Jews and Gentiles.
- Recognize that your old self had to be crucified and buried.
- Recognize you needed redemption.
- Recognize that Jews and Gentiles are saved the same way.
- Admit it: you need God. He loves you and has demonstrated His love.

And then, later in the letter, he begins to disclose some of his motives and expectations. In Romans 11, he said that a motive of his ministry was to make Israel jealous through converting and discipling Gentiles.

> But I am speaking to you who are Gentiles. Inasmuch then as I am an apostle of Gentiles, I magnify my ministry, if somehow I might move to jealousy my fellow countrymen and save some of them. For if their rejection is the reconciliation of the world, what will their acceptance be but life from the dead? (Romans 11:13-15)

Preserving Humility

In Romans, Paul welcomed Gentiles into the family of God without reservation. At the same time, he sought to prevent triumphalism against the Jewish people and preserve the Gentile converts' spiritual stability. Without warning, the apostle left off didactic instruction and broke into inspired metaphor. He began to write about a cultivated Olive Tree, its nourishing root, its vitally connected branches. Paul wrote of cultivated branches broken off, and wild olive branches grafted in among the vitally connected natural branches of this carefully cultivated Tree. The Olive Tree is the Jewish people, from the patriarchs to the present, and their participation in world redemption. The wild olive branches are Gentile believers in Jesus. Towards the end of this instruction, the apostle gave a wonderful revelation of Israel's destiny with a surprising description of this "Tree."

> And they also, if they do not continue in their unbelief, will be grafted in, for God is able to graft them in again. For if you were cut off from what is by nature a wild Olive Tree, and were grafted contrary to nature into a cultivated Olive Tree, how much more will these who are the natural branches be grafted into their own Olive Tree? (Romans 11:23-24)

I'm so glad that these natural branches, despite being broken off, will be easily grafted into their own Olive Tree. They need the Tree. Does this Tree need the broken off branches? I don't know, but I do know that the Tree has an owner and, surprisingly, according to Paul, it's not God. Of course, in the same way everything belongs to God, so does this Olive Tree. Who would want to argue with this? Certainly, not me. All things have their origin, existence and destiny in God.

> For from Him and through Him and to Him are all things. To Him be the glory forever. Amen (Romans 11:36).

However, didn't the language Paul use give another facet of this Tree's identity? It does. He taught that "the Olive Tree" belongs to the "broken off branches." It belongs to natural Israel, both the holy remnant and also unbelieving Jewish people. I would have phrased it differently. I would have said that these broken off branches belonged to the Tree. Paul said the Tree belonged to the branches. There's a difference. Paul dared to remind his readers that what every Christian experiences as they participate in the Kingdom of God belongs to, or originates from, the Jewish people. And this is the shocker: most of them are not connected to what their own God is doing. It is true. They are broken off branches. But it is also true that it is "their own Olive Tree." The Tree belongs to them. It is unique to them. It is theirs. Think about that. This "ownership" was established by Paul to shore up and solidify the respect of Gentile Christians towards the Jewish people. Notice, he was not trying to stir up honor specifically for the Jewish believers in Jesus. He was calling Gentile believers to properly discern unbelieving Jewish people, the broken off natural branches. Gentile Christians were warned to not be arrogant against the Jewish people.

Paul dared to remind his readers that what every Christian experiences as they participate in the Kingdom of God belongs to, or originates from, the Jewish people. And this is the shocker: most of them are not connected to what their own God is doing.

> But if some of the branches were broken off, and you, being a wild olive, were grafted in among them and became partaker with them of the rich

> root of the Olive Tree, do not be arrogant toward the branches; but if you are arrogant, remember that it is not you who supports the root, but the root supports you (Romans 11:17-18).

The root's DNA is indistinguishable from those of the branches which are "broken off." Both root and natural branches are part of the same organism. Of course, we recognize that, throughout the centuries, this admonition was ignored. In 11:24 it says that this Olive Tree was cultivated. The preponderantly Gentile Church cultivated a hybrid of ethnic and theological triumphalism. I find it interesting that the word translated "arrogant toward" has to do with "triumphing over." The historic Gentile Christian vision of superiority and dominance was shortsighted. If they were able to maintain their long-term vision, they'd see this: these broken off natural branches (all of Israel))shall be inserted into their own tree.

Honor

If the Gentile Christians are warned to not be arrogant toward the broken off Jewish branches, what ought their attitude be? The opposite of arrogance is humility, appreciation, and gratitude. From my perspective, the attitude enjoined is "honor." For many, honoring the Jewish people does not come easily. The emotions of wounded self-worth, resentment, and anger may be expressed instead:

> *"I have no need to honor Israel. It is just as much my Olive Tree as theirs. God is just as much my God as He is theirs, and the gospel is just as much ours as theirs... In fact, I am faithful. They are not. I believe. They do not. This Olive Tree is much more mine than it is these, so called, broken off natural branches."*

Although Paul preserved the dignity of every Gentile believer, this arrogant attitude is foreign to his perspective. Paul called for Gentile believers in the Messiah to honor Jesus' identity as "descendant of David",[67] to honor the people from whom Jesus came, to recognize that the Apostolic Community, from whom they received the gospel, saw themselves as part of Israel. Were they wrong? Here's a principle that is age-long:

> But now, I am going to Jerusalem serving the saints. For Macedonia and Achaia have been pleased to make a contribution for the poor among the saints in Jerusalem. Yes, they were pleased to do so, and they are indebted to them. For if the Gentiles have shared in their spiritual things, they are indebted to minister to them also in material things (Romans 15:25-27).

Focus on this: "...if the nations have shared in their spiritual things..." (Romans 15:27b) What responses often arise from this meditation?

> *That is so first century. It's true that the gospel was to the Jew first. Thank God, that's over with.*
>
> *There is no special honor due the Jewish people because there is no distinction between Jew and Gentile.*
>
> *What is it about, "there is neither Jew nor Greek," that you don't get?*

I'm tempted to leave this type of attitude alone. "Well... alrighty then. Have it your way," and wash my hands of the matter. However, I'm trying to build up a New Testament understanding of God's love for the Jewish people, and in good conscience I cannot allow that subliminal, or openly expressed, attitude to remain unchallenged. Read Paul, again.

> For if the Gentiles have shared in their spiritual things, they are indebted to minister to them also in material things (Romans 15:27b).

The Principle of Honor

The One who deserves all honor is God, Himself. We are also called to honor others. Why? We are to recognize and respect the means God employs to shape, preserve, and guide us. He works through intermediaries. If God is the Potter and you are clay, who are God's hands?

- We honor parents: They are the primary instruments God used to create and form us.
- We honor the aged: God has worked through them. They helped establish the culture in which we were raised.
- We honor civil government: God establishes them. They preserve the order in which we may flourish.
- We honor all people: Our interaction with them helps form our character and develop our God-given gifts and callings.
- And, by the way, Paul said that believing Gentiles are called to honor the Jewish people.

Why? Because God shared the Jewish people's spiritual possessions with Gentile believers to spiritually enrich them. Honor the Jewish people? Yes. It is written that those who honor them will be honored (Genesis 12:3). God will bless those who bless them.

When Paul urged Gentile believers to contribute to the poor of the saints of Jerusalem, he appealed to their sense of honor. He did not appeal to the Gentile believers' love for Jewish believers. Nor did he appeal to the Gentile believers' compassion for the suffering poor. In Romans (as opposed to 1 Corinthians), Paul did not encourage Gentile believers to take advantage of an opportunity to bountifully sow and reap finances. The Apostle to the Gentiles appealed to the principle of honor.

From his perspective, the Jewish believers were worthy of help. This is not a matter of giving alms, but of physically repaying an ongoing spiritual debt. This is as foreign to us as Paul calling in a favor from Philemon. This is as bold as the apostle declaring that those who receive the ministry of the Word should support those who minister to them. Paul dared to make this analogous to "sowing to the Spirit."

> The one who is taught the word is to share all good things with the one who teaches him. Do not be deceived, God is not mocked; for whatever a man sows, this he will also reap. For the one who sows to his own flesh will from the flesh reap corruption, but the one who sows to the Spirit will from the Spirit reap eternal life (Galatians 6:6-8).

Look at the principle of supporting "ministers."

> The elders who rule well are to be considered worthy of double honor, especially those who work hard at preaching and teaching. For the Scripture says, "YOU SHALL NOT MUZZLE THE OX WHILE HE IS THRESHING," and "The laborer is worthy of his wages" (1 Timothy 5:17-18).

In this context, "honor" was a euphemism for financial support. Paul called for more than utilitarian maintenance; he called for blessing. That is what "double honor" means. This is what Paul stressed concerning local ministry. Relying upon the same principle, he called for the same response. The Gentile believers were beneficiaries of the overflow of Israel's spiritual blessings.

> For if the Gentiles have shared in their spiritual things, they are indebted to minister to them also in material things (Romans 15:27b).

According to the Apostle Paul, the Gentiles who are flourishing in New Covenant reality are called to see themselves as gratefully receiving the spiritual things of the Jewish people. They are experiencing spiritual abundance because, according to God's will, the Jewish people are sharing the glory of their Messiah with them. Paul encouraged them to think about their redemption in a way that did not usurp Israel's election, but spiritually connected them to the Jewish people. Consequently, the Gentiles were to maintain humility, to show honor, recognizing that it is the Jewish people's "own Olive Tree."

According to the Apostle Paul, the Gentiles who are flourishing in New Covenant reality are called to see themselves as gratefully receiving the spiritual things of the Jewish people.

Is it the Gentile believers' Olive Tree, too? In a sense, yes. They really are wonderfully grafted in among the natural branches. The graft has gloriously taken, and these branches are now receiving the life of this cultivated Olive Tree. Although its origin did not begin with them, it is now their tree too as they gratefully receive the life of Israel's Tree. Paul promised that these wild olive branches would continue to flourish as long as they did not become arrogant against the natural branches.

> Do not be arrogant toward the branches; but if you are arrogant, remember that it is not you who

> supports the root, but the root supports you. You will say then, "Branches were broken off so that I might be grafted in." Quite right, they were broken off for their unbelief, but you stand by your faith. Do not be conceited, but fear; for if God did not spare the natural branches, He will not spare you, either (Romans 11:18-21).

The grafting in of wild olive branches "in among" (11:17) the natural branches is similar to the participation of Gentiles in the "Commonwealth of Israel." They are fellow citizens with the saints, the Jewish Remnant followers of Jesus. As they embrace their identity with the God of Israel through the Jewish Messiah, and thus partake of the Jewish people's covenant relationship, they become holy ones, too. Paul warned the Gentile believers to not boast in their relationship with God against the natural branches who are "broken off." He actually warned them of coming consequences if they did. In the humble King's Commonwealth, it is important to preserve honor. There was tension between Gentile Christian Romans and Messianic Jewish Romans (the Remnant). Interacting with this stress, Paul emphasized both groups mutual need for redemption, called them to loving unity and mutual participation, reminded them of their common eschatological hope, and celebrated diversity with priority.

> Again, he says, "REJOICE, O GENTILES, WITH HIS PEOPLE" (Romans 15:10).

Concerning these Gentile believers, they are beloved friends. They are lovingly grafted in among the beloved natural branches, the believing Jewish people. Concerning the entire Jewish people, beloved for the sake of the patriarchs, it is "their own Olive Tree."[68] God's loving loyalty to Israel is reflected in Paul's inspired priorities. Paul made certain that the church at Rome maintained the original apostolic understanding that Gentile believers participate in the Jewish people's "Olive Tree," partaking of Israel's spiritual riches. God's love for the Jewish people is so intense that even if "branches" are "broken off" because of unfaithfulness, He does not reject them, and God identifies His work in the earth with these people. According to Paul, there is coming a day when they will take possession of their own Olive Tree, being re-grafted, bearing fruit, and receiving the benefits of the life which is rightfully theirs.

Until then, the Gentile Church is reminded to maintain honor and to live in such a way that their intercession for all Israel's salvation is adorned with humility and service. Humility? Yes. It is Israel's "Tree." Service? Again, yes, for they are called to manifest gratitude as seen in financially helping Jewish believers, for they have received of Israel's spiritual wealth.

The Gentile Church is reminded to maintain honor and to live in such a way that their intercession for all Israel's salvation is adorned with humility and service.

What does this say of God's love for the Jewish people? At the least, it communicates an abiding interest in maintaining Israel's dignity, even in the midst of the current estrangement. The fact that God's "Olive Tree" still belongs to them assures us of an everlasting faithfulness which is born of His love for His people.

13

The Sheep and the Goats

The Judgment of the Gentiles (Matthew 25:31-46)

THIS CHAPTER IS ABOUT A PROPHECY THAT PERTAINS to a coming judgment. Its fulfillment will be immediately prior to a fuller manifestation of the Messianic Kingdom that Jesus Himself will inaugurate. Here is a summary of the prophecy and some questions about its intent. It is prophesied that the Messiah will return in visible glory. His angels will be with Him. He will take His seat and judge "all the nations" (Matthew 25:32). He gathers and separates "all the nations," or the individuals from "all the nations." These are judged. If it is individuals that are being judged, perhaps their judgment represents the verdict on their respective nations. Although foreign to our culture, it is a biblical truth that representative individuals can carry the destiny of corporate entities.

In the preceding chapter (Matthew 24), through no fault of their own, those of the Messianic Jewish remnant find themselves swept up in their nation's judgment. Matthew 25:31-46 may follow a similar pattern. Perhaps righteous individuals are to be seen as being evaluated within the framework of their nations' corporate judgment. "Righteous Lot"[69] was affected by Sodom's judgment. Look at Abraham interceding for Lot and his family. These were individuals who lived in a wicked city.

> Far be it from You to do such a thing, to slay the righteous with the wicked, so that the righteous and the wicked are treated alike. Far be it from

> You! Shall not the Judge of all the earth deal justly? (Genesis 18:25)

God is well aware of the godly who live in the midst of ungodly societies. At any rate, the nations (perhaps individuals from those nations) on Messiah's right inherit the Kingdom. Those on His left are sent "into the eternal fire prepared for the devil and his angels" (Matthew 25:41). The judgment is based upon how "all the nations" treated those Jesus called "brethren." The scene does not seem to indicate the general resurrection and subsequent Judgment Day. It is different language; it is something else that may physically foreshadow the ultimate resurrection. Perhaps this is about individuals or nations entering the millennial reign.

The scene does not seem to indicate the general resurrection and subsequent Judgment Day. It is different language; it is something else that may physically foreshadow the ultimate resurrection.

One may ask, what of the "eternal fire?" I find it interesting that in Revelation, just prior to the beginning of "the Millennium,"[70] there is a lake of fire into which the beast and false prophet are cast (Revelation 19:19-21). The Messiah might be prophesying something similar or giving us more information about what John saw. Maybe more than one scene is being viewed at once, and two or more judgments are seen simultaneously.

There is no indication that this is the judgment of all who have ever lived. It is the moment of Jesus' return and His verdict upon "all the nations" and individuals within those nations who are alive at that time. From my perspective, it is not just about individuals, and it is not just about ethnic entities. Somehow, both are involved.

To interpret this prophecy, two crucial questions must be answered. The first is, "Who are Jesus' brethren?" The second, "Who is being judged?"

Who are His brethren?

To interpret this prophecy, one must identify who Jesus was talking about when He said, "these brothers of Mine."[71] Varied alternatives have been offered:

a) the apostles (and thus, by extension, all preachers of the gospel, especially missionaries),

b) all Christians,

c) Jewish disciples in the Great Tribulation,

d) anyone in severe need,

e) the Jewish people.

Some say that the term, "brothers and sisters" of Jesus, fulfills more than one category. For instance, one may believe that a) someone who is a disciple, or b) anyone who is in need, may equally qualify as Jesus' brethren. Throughout Church history, the majority view has been that Jesus' brethren are those who are true believers, or those who preach the gospel.[72] Some teach that this judgment has to do with how one believer treats another when the other is in need. From their perspective, both those who are being judged, and those who were helped are brethren.

Dispensationalists seem to believe that the "brethren" of the Lord are believing Jewish people, or Jewish evangelists, who carry the gospel to the nations during the Great Tribulation.[73] Most responsible exegetes interpret this section of Scripture to signify either all believers, or those who are specifically sent to preach the gospel. Today there are multitudes who apply the passage to anyone who needs practical mercy. We are so used to that interpretation that it comes as a surprise that this was the minority view throughout the centuries.[74]

Our first goal is this: we will try to determine who Jesus' brethren are from the context of the entire Olivet Discourse. Secondly, we need to ask: Who is being judged? The second question will help us clarify the first by the process of elimination.

Who is being judged?

What was the Messiah's emotional state when He prophesied Jerusalem's coming destruction? We can find the answer to that in Matthew and Luke's Gospels. Right before Matthew's Olivet Discourse, we read of the Lord expressing frustration and grief over Jerusalem's rejection and coming calamity.

> "Jerusalem, Jerusalem, who kills the prophets and stones those who are sent to her! How often I wanted to gather your children together, the way a hen gathers her chicks under her wings, and you were unwilling. Behold, your house is being left to you desolate! For I say to you, from now on you will not see Me until you say, 'BLESSED IS HE WHO COMES IN THE NAME OF THE LORD!'"
>
> Jesus came out from the temple and was going away when His disciples came up to point out the temple buildings to Him. And He said to them, "Do you not see all these things? Truly I say to you, not one stone here will be left upon another, which will not be torn down" (Matthew 23:37-24:2).

This same matter is revealed in Luke's parallel passage. We find it shortly before Luke's version of the Olivet prophecy.

> When He approached Jerusalem, He saw the city and wept over it, saying, "If you had known in this day, even you, the things which make for peace! But now they have been hidden from your eyes. For the days will come upon you when your enemies will throw up a barricade against you, and surround you and hem you in on every side, and they will level you to the ground and your children within you, and they will not leave in you one stone upon another, because you did not recognize the time of your visitation" (Luke 19:41-44).

God Incarnate was frustrated. God Incarnate grieved. Jerusalem was not willing (Matthew 23:37). Jerusalem did not recognize (Luke 19:44). Often, these two dynamics are present at the same time. Willingness to do God's will affects the recognition of God's will.[75] Surely such profound emotions did not just evaporate. Jesus prophesied out of the place of emotional pain over the future of His people.

In the beginning of the Olivet Discourse (Matthew 24-25), the grieving Messiah prophesied Jerusalem's temporal, age-long judgment. He foretold Jerusalem's destruction, which transpired in 70 A.D., and the Diaspora that followed. These temporal judgments are the background to a future event. Jesus was not only declaring the immediate future. Within the context of this immediate regional prophecy, the Messiah spoke of His personal, universally visible, glorious return. In Matthew, the prophecies do not end in chapter 24. They proceed into the next chapter. It is possible that the continuation of the Olivet Discourse found in Matthew 25:31-46, may, like Matthew 24, prophesy of the temporal judgment of nations, as well as the eternal judgment of individuals. However, most believe the "separation of the sheep from the goats" prophecy is about the final judgment and pertains solely to individuals. They believe it has nothing to do with the nations' destinies. The prophecy is a bit perplexing, thus the diverse opinions.

Who are, "all the nations?"

There is a way to discover the intention of this oracle. First, identify who "all the nations" are. Next, compare that with the identity of Jesus' brethren. The Messiah's brethren are definitely not numbered amongst "all the nations." After all, the judgment is about how "all the nations" treated His "brethren."

To contrast this, I researched the Septuagint and then looked into the New Testament to identify every verse which includes the phrase, "*panta ta ethne*," "all the nations." To make sure I didn't miss anything, I looked up the phrase, "the nations." As a result, I found that these words do not ever, not even once, specifically refer to the Jewish people. However, they are found in connection to Israel. Here are four examples from the ancient Greek translation of the Hebrew Scriptures, the Septuagint. I will footnote whenever the exact Greek phrase used in Matthew "*panta ta ethne*" is found.

Through Abraham "all the nations" shall be blessed.

> But Abraam shall become a great and populous nation, and in him shall all the nations[76] of the earth be blest (Genesis 18:18 LXE).

The God of Israel shall scatter His people among "all the nations."

> And the Lord thy God shall scatter thee among all (the) nations,[77] from one end of the earth to the other; and thou shalt there serve other gods, wood and stone, which thou hast not known, nor thy fathers (Deuteronomy 28:64 LXE).

"All the nations" shall inquire about God's motive for Israel's scattering and their Land's desolation.

> And all the nations[78] shall say, "Why has the Lord done thus to this land? What is this great fierceness of anger?" (Deuteronomy 29:24 LXE)

In the first Diaspora, it was said that the Jewish people's laws differed from those of "all the nations."

> And he spoke to king Artaxerxes, saying, "There is a nation scattered among the nations in all thy kingdom, and their laws differ from those of all the other nations;[79] and they disobey the laws of the king; and it is not expedient for the king to let them alone" (Esther 3:8 LXE).

This phrase is used about seventy times in the Septuagint.[80] The overwhelming majority of these verses distinctly contrast Israel with "all the nations."

Are we to believe that this did not inform the Messiah's language or worldview? Might we be expected to surmise that the author of Matthew was ignorant of the Bible he quoted and upon which he relied? Jesus and Matthew were not biblically illiterate, and in the Bible, "the nations," or, "all the nations," means, "the Gentiles," as differentiated from the Jewish people, or, "all the Gentiles" in contrast to Israel. The word "nations" is interchangeable with, translated as, "Gentiles." In the prophecy of the sheep and the goats, the Gentile nations are gathered.

> *In the prophecy of the sheep and the goats, the Gentile nations are gathered.*

Despite the biblical data, some people I know might reflexively remonstrate,

> *Wait! Do you dare to declare that "all the nations" Jesus gathers for judgment does not include the Jewish people?*
>
> *Don't you believe Jews need Jesus?*

Yes, the gospel is for Jewish people.[81] However, in this unique context, I believe the Jewish people are being delivered from the unrighteous wrath of the nations, and not gathered for judgment together with them.

> It will come about in that day that I will make Jerusalem a heavy stone for all the peoples; all who lift it will be severely injured. And all the nations (*panta ta ethne*) of the earth will be gathered against it...Then the LORD will go forth and fight against those nations, as when He fights on a day of battle (Zechariah 12:3; 14:3).

From time immemorial, a distinction was made between Israel and all the nations. Here is a seminal oracle:

> As I see him from the top of the rocks, and I look at him from the hills; behold, a people who dwells apart, and will not be reckoned among the nations (Numbers 23:9).

Israel is not part of this assembly. At the end of the age their separate nature and unique relationship to Jesus is fully revealed and the nations are shocked.

> Then the righteous will answer Him, "Lord, when did we see You hungry, and feed You, or thirsty, and give You something to drink? And when did we see You a stranger, and invite You in, or naked, and clothe You? When did we see You sick, or in prison, and come to You?" The King will answer and say to them, "Truly I say to you, to the extent that you did it to one of these brothers of Mine, even the least of them, you did it to Me" (Matthew 25:37-40).

The nations' resentment against God's election of Israel results in the nations' determination to ensure that Israel is seen as the same as any other nation. This attitude is revealed in one of Jeremiah's prophetic indictments of Moab together with a divinely determined consequence.

> *The nations' resentment against God's election of Israel results in the nations' determination to ensure that Israel is seen as the same as any other nation.*

> Thus saith the Lord; "Because Moab has said, 'Behold, are not the house of Israel and Juda like all the other nations?'[82] Therefore, behold, I will weaken the shoulder of Moab from his frontier cities, even the choice land, the house of Bethasimuth above the fountain of the city, by the sea-side" (Ezekiel 25:8-9 LXE).

From the time of Abram's calling, his God decreed a curse upon those who trivialize Israel's election (Genesis 12:3). Devaluing the descendants of Abraham, Isaac and Jacob provokes God. It makes light of His choice and disregards His majesty. It prepares the way for the maltreatment of those who are "beloved for the sake of the patriarchs" while they are dispersed amongst the nations.

The carnal mind reasons,

> *"Why not? They're like any other people. There are no divinely determined consequences for how we treat the Jews."*

Summation:

The nations' treatment of the Jewish people is a test all nations must endure. The Jewish people have been scattered amongst many peoples. How were they treated during what has rightly been called "the Diaspora?" A sober assessment of end-time prophecy leads many to believe there will be an ultimate end time test of "all the nations" which test those nations will fail. They shall gather together to fight against the Jewish people, many of whom (or, all of whom) have been regathered to the Promised Land.[83] Read this.

> Let them be aroused, let all the nations go up to the valley of Josaphat: for there will I sit to judge all the Gentiles (*panta ta ethne*) round about (Joel 3:12 LXE).

The Olivet Discourse framed the believing communities' perspective of the imminent judgment of Jerusalem. The outcome of this destruction was the Diaspora Jesus prophesied. The Jewish people's presence among the nations is due to this judgment. The identity, separation, and destiny of sheep and goats shall be determined by the way "all the nations" treated the Jewish people during the millennia of exile. It seems like Jewish people have been scattered to practically "all the nations" on earth. Certainly, the Covenant Curses (Deuteronomy 28:64) have been dreadfully, rigorously fulfilled. The prophesied judgment on "all the nations" shall also be fulfilled.

Allow me to gently offer my perspective.

Matthew 25:40 speaks of when, at the parousia, the Messiah gathers all the Gentiles, and judges them according to the way they treated His brethren. The prophets proclaim this principle. Obadiah made this plain concerning Edom, a nation adverse to Israel that typifies the attitude of "all the nations."

> "Do not enter the gate of My people in the day of their disaster. Yes, you, do not gloat over their calamity in the day of their disaster. And do not loot their wealth in the day of their disaster. Do not stand at the fork of the road to cut down their fugitives; and do not imprison their survivors in

> the day of their distress. For the day of the LORD draws near on all the nations.[84] As you have done, it will be done to you. Your dealings will return on your own head (Obadiah 1:13-15).

Matthew 25:31-46 follows prophecies of Jerusalem's doom and the coming Diaspora (Matthew 23:34-24). This oracle is best interpreted through that lens. Those who understand that to be a major theme of Mark 13, Luke 21, and Matthew 24 may have the easiest time seeing that the judgment of "all the nations" is related to the way the Jewish people were treated in their midst as a result of that scattering. This context dictates that the measure of reward or punishment is commensurate to how these nations treated Israel in the Jewish people's time of weakness and need.

> *The measure of reward or punishment is commensurate to how these nations treated Israel in the Jewish people's time of weakness and need.*

Some may mistakenly identify this interpretation with Dispensationalism and dismiss it out of hand. In fact, Dispensationalism does not propound what I am offering for your consideration. They believe these Scriptures refer to the way "all the nations" will receive or reject "the 144,000 Jewish evangelists" during "the Great Tribulation" subsequent to the pre-tribulation rapture of the Church. I believe that what I am proposing comes from the context of Jesus' prediction of the scattering of the Jewish people, His brethren.

Here's an example of someone who came to the same conclusion. Hans Kung[85] is a Roman Catholic theologian. He was influenced by neo-orthodoxy. He is about as far away from Dispensationalism as possible. He wrote:

> The Church preached love, while it sowed the seeds of murderous hatred; it proclaimed love, while it prepared the way for atrocities and death.

> And these acts were perpetrated against the compatriots and brothers of him who taught the Church: "What you did to one of the least of these my brethren, you did to me." ...The Church that stood between Israel and Jesus prevented Israel from recognizing its Messiah.[86]

I would never say that the Messiah could not possibly be speaking as the Son of Man vis-à-vis His relationship to all humanity. It is also a valuable application to see Jesus as Head of the Church, and Brother to every believer. Perhaps there is a foreshadowing of this holy identification in Jesus' encounter with Paul.

> "Saul, Saul, why are you persecuting Me?" And he said, "Who are You, Lord?" And He said, "I am Jesus whom you are persecuting" (Acts 9:4b-5).

At the same time, I have concluded that despite all these worthy applications, there should be a priority in interpretation. Again, this prophecy most likely refers to Jesus the Conqueror calling the Gentile nations to account. It follows closely on the heels of His prophecy of the Jewish people's coming calamity. Jesus the Messiah's identity as the Brother can be seen within the context of the title He bore as He suffered and died for the redemption of the nations: "King of the Jews." During His suffering and throughout Israel's sufferings in the Diaspora, Jesus identifies with the Jewish people.

From my perspective, the gathering of "all the nations" to stand before the King is the ultimate fulfillment of the original oracle concerning Abraham and his descendants.

> And I will make you a great nation, and I will bless you, and make your name great; and so you shall be a blessing; and I will bless those who bless you, and the one who curses you I will curse. And in you all the families of the earth will be blessed (Genesis 12:2-3).

Ultimately, the way the peoples relate to the Jews is the way they relate to the King of the Jews. The way they relate to the seed of Abraham, Isaac, and Jacob[87] is the way they relate to the Seed of Abraham, Jesus the Messiah.[88]

> The King will answer and say to them, "Truly I say to you, to the extent that you did it to one of these brothers of Mine, even the least of them, you did it to Me."
>
> Then He will answer them, "Truly I say to you, to the extent that you did not do it to one of the least of these, you did not do it to Me" (Matthew 25:40, 45).

The Prophecy

Here is the prophecy. Experiment and read it along the lines of what I suggest. You may come away with a heightened appreciation for Jesus' loyalty to His people. The only change I suggest is reading "all the nations" in the way "*panta ta ethne*" has always been translated: "all the Gentiles." It changes the way the whole prophecy is commonly understood. It is found in verse Matthew 25:32a.

> All the Gentiles will be gathered before Him...

From the beginning:

> But when the Son of Man comes in His glory, and all the angels with Him, then He will sit on His glorious throne. All the Gentiles will be gathered before Him; and He will separate them from one another, as the shepherd separates the sheep from the goats; and He will put the sheep on His right, and the goats on the left.
>
> Then the King will say to those on His right, "Come, you who are blessed of My Father, inherit the kingdom prepared for you from the foundation

> of the world. For I was hungry, and you gave Me something to eat; I was thirsty, and you gave Me something to drink; I was a stranger, and you invited Me in; naked, and you clothed Me; I was sick, and you visited Me; I was in prison, and you came to Me."
>
> Then the righteous will answer Him, "Lord, when did we see You hungry, and feed You, or thirsty, and give You something to drink? And when did we see You a stranger, and invite You in, or naked, and clothe You? When did we see You sick, or in prison, and come to You?"
>
> The King will answer and say to them, "Truly I say to you, to the extent that you did it to one of these brothers of Mine, even the least of them, you did it to Me."
>
> Then He will also say to those on His left, "Depart from Me, accursed ones, into the eternal fire which has been prepared for the devil and his angels; for I was hungry, and you gave Me nothing to eat; I was thirsty, and you gave Me nothing to drink; I was a stranger, and you did not invite Me in; naked, and you did not clothe Me; sick, and in prison, and you did not visit Me."
>
> Then they themselves also will answer, "Lord, when did we see You hungry, or thirsty, or a stranger, or naked, or sick, or in prison, and did not take care of You?"
>
> Then He will answer them, "Truly I say to you, to the extent that you did not do it to one of the least of these, you did not do it to Me."
>
> These will go away into eternal punishment, but the righteous into eternal life (Matthew 25:31-46).

In Matthew 25, as in the rest of the Scriptures, "all the nations"[89] means "all the Gentiles." There is no reason to change the meaning of this phrase, and there are compelling reasons to maintain consistency in what these words meant.

At this judgment, the Lord continues to distinguish between His people and the rest of humanity. Israel is "loved for the sake of the Patriarchs" (Romans 11:28b). God, through Israel's Messiah, loves the whole world.

My goal is to look into God's love for the Jewish people through the eyes of the New Testament. The "Parable of the Sheep and the Goats" illustrates that love. Consider the loyalty of God Incarnate to the people through whom He became flesh (Romans 9:5). Isn't He wonderful?

Behold, the Lion that
IS
from the tribe of Judah
(Revelation 5:5)

Verses List:

For those who are interested, here is the list of verses where the phrase "*panta ta ethne*" (all the nations) is found in the Septuagint (including the Apocrypha) and the New Testament. It is found 104 times.

Gen 18:18; 22:18; 26:4; Exod 23:27; 33:16; Deut 7:6f, 14; 10:15; 11:23; 28:10, 64; 29:23; Josh 4:24; 23:4; 24:18; 1 Sam 8:20; 1 Chr 14:17; 2 Chr 33:9; 1 Esd 5:49; Neh 6:16; Esth 3:8; Jdt 3:8; Tob 14:6; Tbs. 14:6; 1 Macc 1:42; 2:18f; 4:11; 5:38, 43; 12:53; 13:6; 3 Macc 7:4; Ps 9:18; 46:2; 48:2; 58:6, 9; 71:11, 17; 85:9; 112:4; 116:1; 117:10; Odes 7:37; Sir 36:1; Pss. Sol. 9:9; 17:34; Amos 9:12; Joel 4:2, 11f; Obad 1:15f; Hab 2:5; Hag 2:7; Zech 7:14; 12:3, 9; 14:2, 18; Mal 2:9; 3:12; Isa 2:2; 14:12, 26; 25:7; 34:2; 40:15, 17; 43:9; 66:18; Jer 3:17; 9:25; 25:9; 32:13, 15; 43:2; Ezek 25:8; 38:16; 39:21, 23; Dan 3:2, 7, 37; 7:14; Dat. 3:37; Matt 25:32; 28:19; Mark 13:10; Luke 12:30;

24:47; Acts 14:16; 15:17; Rom 15:11; 16:26; Gal 3:8; 2 Tim 4:17; Rev 12:5; 14:8; 15:4; 18:3, 23

14

The Redeemer, Part 1: He Shall Come

HERE IS GOD'S HEART FOR THE JEWISH PEOPLE:

> For I know the plans that I have for you, declares the LORD, plans for welfare and not for calamity to give you a future and a hope (Jeremiah 29:11).

Our topic remains the revelation of God's love for the Jewish people in the New Testament. Relying upon the Hebrew Scriptures, the New Testament is not silent on this matter. Paul, the Apostle to the Nations, is especially clear about this in Romans. There is a small portion in Romans that is often overlooked. It is dwarfed by its context. This section is Romans 11:26b-27. Unless you're very familiar with this section, you probably won't notice that it's missing from this passage.

> For I do not want you, brethren, to be uninformed of this mystery—so that you will not be wise in your own estimation—that a partial hardening has happened to Israel until the fullness of the Gentiles has come in; and so all Israel will be saved; just as it is written...From the standpoint of the gospel they are enemies for your sake, but from the standpoint of God's choice they are beloved for the sake of the fathers; for the gifts and the calling of God are irrevocable (Romans 11:25-26a, 28-29).

Explosive Revelations

In these verses, Paul drops theological bombshells that startle me in their boldness and clarity. When I read this section, the following is what grabs my attention.

First: "A partial hardening has happened to Israel until the fullness of the Gentiles comes in." Paul prophesies that there's a time limit to majority Israel's unbelief. As a result, "all Israel shall be saved!" What an amazing prophecy. (Then there is the overlooked section. Most do not emphasize it. I certainly haven't.)

Continuing to read, my attention is recaptured... Paul wrote, during this time of "partial hardening" God is devoted to them for the sake of their patriarchs. Finally, Paul underscored that the Jewish people's gifts and callings are irrevocable. In Romans 11:25-29, Paul began to conclude his majestic prophetic instruction concerning God's relationship to Israel. These unexpected insights are staggering. They reveal the merciful consummation of God's interaction with Israel. As I mentioned, in my casual reading, I tend to skip Paul's underemphasized passage:

> *Paul began to conclude his majestic prophetic instruction concerning God's relationship to Israel. These unexpected insights are staggering.*

> THE DELIVERER WILL COME FROM ZION, HE WILL REMOVE UNGODLINESS FROM JACOB. THIS IS MY COVENANT WITH THEM, WHEN I TAKE AWAY THEIR SINS (Romans 11:26b-27).

When you read the passage, did you notice it was missing? In the past, for me, it would not have mattered whether verses 26b-27 were there or not. Obviously, it mattered to Paul. What does it mean? How does it fit? What does it reveal about God's heart? What was Paul stressing? He was stressing the Messiah. Israel's salvation does not happen automatically. It takes Jesus' personal involvement. Here is the immediate context of our study. It is the beginning of the home stretch of Paul's instruction in Romans 11.

> For I do not want you, brethren, to be uninformed of this mystery—so that you will not be wise in your own estimation—that a partial hardening has happened to Israel until the fullness of the Gentiles has come in; and so all Israel will be saved; just as it is written,
>
> "THE DELIVERER WILL COME FROM ZION, HE WILL REMOVE UNGODLINESS FROM JACOB. THIS IS MY COVENANT WITH THEM, WHEN I TAKE AWAY THEIR SINS."
>
> From the standpoint of the gospel they are enemies for your sake, but from the standpoint of God's choice they are beloved for the sake of the fathers; for the gifts and the calling of God are irrevocable (Romans 11:25-29).

Some believe that "and so all Israel shall be saved" is a summation of what was immediately, previously, written.

That interpretation looks like this: "A partial hardening has happened to Israel until the fullness of the Gentiles has come in; and so all Israel will be saved." They believe that the "Israel" which "will be saved" is the transgenerational Church. They believe this Church is comprised of all the Gentiles who have been saved (the fullness of which has finally "come in") and Jews who have been saved through the millenia.

A small minority believes "and so all Israel will be saved" refers to the sum of the Jewish remnant who were saved throughout the millennia.

However, the phrase "and so all Israel will be saved" is intended to be introductory to the rest of the sentence. This sentence contains a prophecy of a future crisis and deliverance. Here is the entire section:

> And so all Israel will be saved, just as it is written, "THE DELIVERER WILL COME FROM ZION, HE WILL REMOVE UNGODLINESS FROM JACOB. THIS IS MY COVENANT WITH THEM, WHEN I TAKE AWAY THEIR SINS" Romans 11:26-27).

It is obvious that "just as it is written" is not the end of a sentence. That phrase introduces the Old Testament quote. The reference reveals Israel's prophesied salvation and the renewal of covenant relationship. Paul is using a form of "spiritual shorthand." When he writes of the future covenant God shall make with Jacob, he is referencing Israel's entry into the experience of the New Covenant. Isaiah elaborates upon this covenantal transgenerational relationship in chapter 59. He reveals the aftermath of the covenant's inauguration in the following chapter (Isaiah 60).

What happens after Israel's national salvation? Paul wrote, it shall be "life from the dead" (Romans 11:15). What does "life from the dead" look like? Does it have any reference to Israel? Is it a promise of a restored cosmos that has nothing to do with the Jewish people except, perhaps, peripherally? Hidden within the reiteration of this ancient prophecy is an indication of what Israel's salvation entails.

"[And] so all Israel shall be saved" is a conclusion that functions like a connective. It links two sides of the same process. Let me explain. "[A]ll Israel" being saved happens at some time after "the fullness of the Gentiles" comes into relationship with Jesus. The long night of Israel's "partial hardening" comes to an end when "the fullness of the

Gentiles" are saved. This "fullness" signals the dawn of a new day when the "partial hardening" is alleviated.

However, Paul's emphasis is upon the means of "all" Israel's salvation. Israel will be saved by the coming Deliverer. He comes at the end of Israel's "partial hardening" which corresponds to when "the fullness of the Gentiles has come in." The precursor to the arrival of the Redeemer is worldwide revival amongst the nations. The return of the Deliverer is the climax of this process. Paul summed up Israel's destiny with a revelation of the Jewish people's restoration. The following chapters focus upon God's heart for Israel revealed in these two verses:

> And so all Israel will be saved; just as it is written: "THE DELIVERER WILL COME FROM ZION, HE WILL REMOVE UNGODLINESS FROM JACOB. THIS IS MY COVENANT WITH THEM, WHEN I TAKE AWAY THEIR SINS" (Romans 11:26-27).

These verses are eschatological. What do they mean? What do we learn about God's heart through them? We'll review these verses, look at some biblical background and offer a view of Paul's expectation. Again, our topic is God's love for Israel as described in the New Testament. Regarding this theme, these verses and their background are relevant and revelatory.

Of Whom Did Paul Prophesy?

Identifying Israel and Jacob.

> HE WILL REMOVE UNGODLINESS FROM JACOB (Romans 11:26b).

Paul outlined the current condition and future history of the Church and Israel. Summing up the process, he wrote, "all Israel will be saved." Who are they?[90] Those who mistakenly celebrate the Church as "Israel" generally believe "all Israel shall be saved" refers to the completion of the Body of Christ. Their perception is that the fullness of the Gentiles coming into the Kingdom is synonymous with the salvation of "all Israel." To these believers, "all Israel" being saved means that the Great Commission is finally accomplished and the end has come. They do not believe there is any future hope for the Jews as a people, or that there will be an end-time "conversion" of the Jewish people who will then be added to the Church, the "true Israel." To them, "Israel" is comprised of the transgenerational, transnational Church. For the supersessionist, Paul did not intend that the designation, "Israel," would have any meaning beyond those who believe in Jesus. These believe that "Israel" does not mean "the Jewish people." To them it means "the Church."

To be consistent with their conclusion, they grapple with this text to wrest it from its context. Astoundingly, they insist that the people-group "Israel," described as being partially hardened (v. 25b), means something completely different than the "all Israel" which shall be saved (v. 26a). Their predetermined theology requires that these semantic contortions take place within the same sentence! Amazing!

Here's the sentence they propose:

> *Israel is partially hardened until the Great Commission is finished and then the whole Church will be saved.*

That is not what Paul wrote. Neither is it what he intended his readers to believc.

Let's walk through these verses and try to give the meaning according to this manner of misinterpretation. Here is a little comic skit with Paul on one side of the stage and another person (who must look dignified) on the other.

Paul: A partial hardening has happened to Israel...

Dr. Misinterpreter: "Israel" here means those Jews who are unbelieving.

Paul: until the fullness of the Gentiles has come in...

Dr. Misinterpreter: God's ultimate goal is the completion of the Great Commission. The fullness of the Gentiles coming in is not a transitional means to an end. It is the end.

Paul: and so all Israel...

Dr. Misinterpreter: "Israel" means the entire transgenerational international Church which is complete when the fullness of the Gentiles come in.

Paul: will be saved; just as it is written, "THE DELIVERER WILL COME FROM ZION...

Dr. Misinterpreter: "Zion" is the heavenly state that has no relationship to earthly "Zion." "Earth-Zion" is a shadow city, and now the Son has risen and the shadows have vanished in the light of the Christ.

Paul: HE WILL REMOVE UNGODLINESS FROM JACOB...

Dr. Misinterpreter: (Grumble, grumble... mutters under his breath) Whoever "Jacob" is, (grumpy grumble) let's skip that...well...Let's see...this is puzzling...Aha! (Cheering up) I have seen my way through this conundrum. Here is the answer to the mysterious code of what "Jacob" means:

(Ahem, ahem...clearing throat, speaking with dignity...)

To be consistent with Paul's theology of the Church, which has taken the place of ethnic Israel, of necessity, "Jacob" must mean "the Church."

Paul: "THIS IS MY COVENANT WITH THEM, WHEN I TAKE AWAY THEIR SINS."

Dr. Misinterpreter: This is painful because it makes no sense. This has already happened to all who believe. The Church is already cleansed from sin. It must mean, "I have already taken away their sins." Someone must have sneakily changed the Bible. I'll bet that in the original manuscripts it read, "I have already taken away the Church's sins."

Paul: From the standpoint of the gospel, they are enemies for your sake...

Dr. Misinterpreter: That means the first use of the name "Israel," who are the unbelieving Jews. You have to be very nimble to follow Paul. He constantly, and without warning (!), changes definitions of the same word in the same paragraph.

Oh, yes. They are enemies. (Beginning to froth at the mouth...) Enemies of humanity, enemies of God, enemies of themselves, enemies of the Church. My enemies! (Calling for a pogrom) Your enemies!

Paul: but from the standpoint of God's choice...

Dr. Misinterpreter: Obviously, the Church is the chosen people. "God's Choice" defines "spiritual "Israel,"

Paul: they are beloved for the sake of the fathers...

Dr. Misinterpreter: Maybe that means all true Christians because, obviously, God cannot be concerned with physical ancestors or descendants.

A maxim of New Testament Interpretation is: "Matter, inferior. Spirit, superior." Ask any philosopher.

Paul: for the gifts and the calling of God are irrevocable (Romans 11:25-29).

Dr. Misinterpreter: We know that this cannot mean what it seems to say, so skip this too, except if it refers to a minister who has fallen into gross sin.

Question: How do they manage to mangle the meaning of these Scriptures with a clear conscience?

Answer: Centuries of misappropriating Israel's identity make it the path of least resistance. It is part of the culture and self-identity of the Church.

Centuries of misappropriating Israel's identity make it the path of least resistance. It is part of the culture and self-identity of the Church.

15

The Redeemer, Part 2: Twisting Paul's Words

THE INTERPRETERS MENTIONED IN THE PREVIOUS chapter misidentify the "Israel" which shall be saved through other misconstrued verses. They primarily rely upon two earlier statements in Romans. They believe these verses are self-evident means of interpretation which theologically unsophisticated yahoos mistakenly gloss over. Are they right? Let's review them.

The first section misused to interpret "Israel" is in the opening chapters of Romans wherein the "true Jew" is designated.

> For he is not a Jew who is one outwardly, nor is circumcision that which is outward in the flesh. But he is a Jew who is one inwardly; and circumcision is that which is of the heart, by the Spirit, not by the letter; and his praise is not from men, but from God (Romans 2:28-29).

Next, people who mistakenly identify "Israel" with the Church rely heavily upon Romans 9:6.

> But it is not as though the word of God has failed. For they are not all Israel who are descended from Israel; nor are they all children because they are Abraham's descendants, but: "THROUGH ISAAC YOUR DESCENDANTS WILL BE NAMED" (Romans 9:6-7).

In both portions of Scripture, a distinction is made between those who are "merely" physically descended from Abraham, Isaac, and Jacob and those Jewish people who have been "born of God." Paul is describing Israel's godly remnant. However, when supersessionists read, "and so all Israel shall be saved," they often default to these verses and redefine Israel as the Church.

Here is a reasonably fair satiric encapsulation of things I've read and conversations I've had:

> *Would you please look at what Paul wrote about the Jews in 2:28-29 and 9:6?*
>
> *See?*
>
> *"All Israel shall be saved" is not talking about Jews. It is referring to all who have been born of the Spirit.*
>
> *Paul's understanding of "Israel" is that all who are "circumcised" in their "hearts" are Jews. Not those who are merely Jews "according to the flesh."*
>
> *We Christians are the true "Jews."*
>
> *Not all Israel is, "Israel."*
>
> *"Israel" is a code word, an enigma hidden in a mystery. What does the metaphor "Israel" mean?*
>
> *"Israel" means "us."*

Somehow it always comes down to this:

> *"Israel" means "the Church"*
>
> *And we are "the Church"*
>
> *And "the Church" is us*
>
> *And therefore we are "Israel."*

What's missing in their calculations? The remnant.

The Remnant.

Somehow, it escapes their attention that Paul believed in a distinctly Jewish, saved remnant. Paul wrote of the Messianic Jewish remnant in these passages, not of ethnically amorphous believers. The remnant is comprised of those Jews who are spiritually alive in the Messiah. They are physically and spiritually Israel. Both sacred spiritual and holy material reality combine in these people. Can such a thing be? Certainly. The quintessential expression of this unity is the Incarnation. Later in Romans, Paul further explains his understanding of the remnant.

The first place Paul clarified his understanding of the remnant is in Romans 9:27-29 (following, and further explaining, 9:6b: "For they are not all Israel who are descended from Israel"). Paul distinguished those who come under God's judgment and those who are mercifully spared.

> Isaiah cries out concerning Israel,
>
> "THOUGH THE NUMBER OF THE SONS OF ISRAEL BE LIKE THE SAND OF THE SEA, IT IS THE REMNANT THAT WILL BE SAVED; FOR THE LORD WILL EXECUTE HIS WORD ON THE EARTH, THOROUGHLY AND QUICKLY."
>
> And just as Isaiah foretold,
>
> "UNLESS THE LORD OF SABAOTH HAD LEFT TO US A POSTERITY, WE WOULD HAVE BECOME LIKE SODOM, AND WOULD HAVE RESEMBLED GOMORRAH" (Romans 9:27-29).

That passage should have been enough to express Paul's perspective of the remnant. The remnant is the saved "sons of Israel." However, he drove his point home as he elaborated upon the remnant in the beginning of Romans 11. Please note verse 5.

> God has not rejected His people whom He foreknew. Or do you not know what the Scripture says in the passage about Elijah, how he pleads with God against Israel?
>
> "Lord, THEY HAVE KILLED YOUR PROPHETS, THEY HAVE TORN DOWN YOUR ALTARS, AND I ALONE AM LEFT, AND THEY ARE SEEKING MY LIFE."
>
> But what is the divine response to him?
>
> "I HAVE KEPT for Myself SEVEN THOUSAND MEN WHO HAVE NOT BOWED THE KNEE TO BAAL."
>
> In the same way then, there has also come to be at the present time a remnant according to God's gracious choice (Romans 11:2-5).

My questions for those who, relying upon Romans 2:28-29 and 9:6-7, contend that "Israel" is the Church are the following:

1. Didn't Paul know what he believed about Israel's Remnant when he wrote those (earlier) verses?

2. Shouldn't we take into consideration his teaching about the remnant when he discusses the identity of the Israel that is "true Israel?"

In Romans, "Israel" meant "Israel." Paul was not using "Israel" as a cypher for "The Church." He was not trying to confuse those with whom he corresponded. He didn't speak of Israel as the Jewish people in one part of a sentence and then redefine Israel as the Church in the very next phrase of the very same sentence. Let's read the passage again.

Paul was not trying to confuse those with whom he corresponded. He didn't speak of Israel as the Jewish people in one part of a sentence and then redefine Israel as the Church in the very next phrase of the very same sentence.

> For I do not want you, brethren, to be uninformed of this mystery-- so that you will not be wise in your own estimation-- that a partial hardening has happened to Israel until the fullness of the Gentiles has come in; and so all Israel will be saved; just as it is written,
>
> "THE DELIVERER WILL COME FROM ZION, HE WILL REMOVE UNGODLINESS FROM JACOB."
>
> "THIS IS MY COVENANT WITH THEM, WHEN I TAKE AWAY THEIR SINS."
>
> From the standpoint of the gospel they are enemies for your sake, but from the standpoint of God's choice they are beloved for the sake of the fathers; for the gifts and the calling of God are irrevocable (Romans 11:25-29).

Those who have a supersessionist ax to grind have been forced to chop these earlier verses (Romans 2:28-29; 9:6) out of their context, which is the rest of Romans. According to them, what Paul longed to subtly communicate is this: The "all Israel" that "will be saved" is the Church.

To redefine Israel as the Church in this context is absurd. Ordinarily, context determines the meaning of words in a consistent fashion, so the meaning of "Israel" in Romans 11 should not lurch about like a wooden roller coaster. In addition, this mode of interpretation provides a great disservice to the heart and character of our Father. He is faithful, and it is explicitly written that He loves the Jewish people for the sake of the patriarchs (11:28-29).

In 11:25, just before he communicated the astonishing resolution of Israel's alienation, Paul introduced a "mystery" he was about to reveal. Let us rehearse it. Here's the mystery: a partial hardening has happened to the Jewish people that will continue up until the time the fullness of the nations come to faith. When that happens, the hardening stops and Israel gets saved (delivered) because the Redeemer comes.

Paul was not referring to the Church when he prophesied Israel's corporate, complete salvation. Can anyone imagine that the disciples at Rome didn't already believe that the Church was to be saved? Would that be a new revelation? Of course, believers in the Messiah would be saved. That was no mystery. However, to the Gentile Roman disciples, Israel's certain future restoration was. Alas, to many believers, it is still a mystery. They are so alienated from God's heart for His people that they cannot make sense of that which is plainly written.

Hardness of heart has happened to the Church. As the Church has judged, so has it happened to the Church.

Tragically, blindness, in part, has happened to the Church. Hardness of heart has happened to the Church. As the Church has judged, so has it happened to the Church. Paul was not kidding when he wrote,

> Do not be arrogant toward the branches; but if you are arrogant, remember that it is not you who supports the root, but the root supports you.
>
> You will say then, "Branches were broken off so that I might be grafted in."
>
> Quite right, they were broken off for their unbelief, but you stand by your faith. Do not be conceited, but fear; for if God did not spare the natural branches, He will not spare you, either.
>
> Behold then the kindness and severity of God; to those who fell, severity, but to you, God's kindness, if you continue in His kindness; otherwise you also will be cut off (Romans 11:18-22).

Many who are reading this have been taught by the Spirit to embrace God's love for the Jewish people. If that is you, know this: you are in the mainstream of the apostle Paul's revelation and apostolic motivation. You are not an unsophisticated theological lout. You are in harmony with the heart of Paul's God.

"Jacob" means "Israel"

In Romans 11:26 Paul unambiguously taught that "Israel" corresponds to "Jacob." These names are used, in parallel, in the same sentence. We find them in the same verse. They signify the same people. One defines the other.

Is it feasible that the historic predominantly Gentile Church might be in view when Paul references "Jacob?" Is that what the recipients of Paul's letter to the Roman house churches could have understood? Please reread this section:

> "THE DELIVERER WILL COME FROM ZION, HE WILL REMOVE UNGODLINESS FROM JACOB."

> "THIS IS MY COVENANT WITH THEM, WHEN I TAKE AWAY THEIR SINS" (Romans 11:26b-27).

The made-righteous Roman Gentile disciples would not see themselves characterized as the ungodly "Jacob" in these verses. Search as one might, they were not in view here.

Foretelling

In addition, this prophecy is transparently foretelling, not opaquely forth-telling. It references Israel's future, not the church's present. This event is yet to happen. It is not an explanation of a current state with the promise of a greater future fulfillment. There is nothing proleptic about this prophecy except if it is viewed through the lens of the Jewish remnant's salvation. At the risk of being confusing, allow me to state that the "Israel that is Israel" does speak of the future restoration of "Israel." The remnant is God's down payment on the future full redemption of the entire people.

> *The transnational Church was never called "Jacob" and will never be "Jacob." These verses do not speak of the present or future of saved Gentiles. They prophesy the coming salvation of the Jewish people.*

The transnational Church was never called "Jacob" and will never be "Jacob." These verses do not speak of the present or future of saved Gentiles. They prophesy the coming salvation of the Jewish people.

The following "reasoning" is ridiculous:

> *"Israel" means "the Church."*
>
> *"Jacob" means "Israel."*
>
> *Therefore, "Jacob" means "the Church."*

Since we are "the Church," we are "Jacob."

Paul prophesied according to the Scriptures, and in this reiterated oracle (Isaiah 59:20-21), the Jewish people's complete restoration is foreseen and foretold.

Who was Jacob?

Jacob was an elect man who needed to be transformed. At the time of his transformation he was in a dire situation. His crisis reflects the Jewish people's future. Esau threatened Jacob's life. So shall Israel's existence be threatened by surrounding nations.[91] Jacob encountered a hostile covenant partner, the Angel of the LORD. They fought throughout the night. At dawn, at the end of that conflict, Jacob attained victory through his own defeat. As a result, he was renewed and renamed.

> He said, "Your name shall no longer be Jacob, but Israel; for you have striven with God and with men and have prevailed" (Genesis 32:28).

Here is the prophet Hosea's commentary on this episode:

> The LORD also has a dispute with Judah, and will punish Jacob according to his ways; He will repay him according to his deeds. In the womb he took his brother by the heel, and in his maturity he contended with God.
>
> Yes, he wrestled with the angel and prevailed; He wept and sought His favor. He found Him at Bethel and there He spoke with us, even the LORD, the God of hosts, The LORD is His name (Hosea 12:2-5).

Paul predicted something similar. Majority Israel, a people who (God be merciful!) are described as disobedient, obstinate, partially hardened, insensate, blind, deaf, distracted, enslaved, broken off, unbelieving, hostile to the gospel (Romans 10:21; 11:7-10, 17, 23, 28) are like Jacob. Like Jacob, they will wrestle with their King throughout the dark night of this age until the dawn of the next. Corporate "Jacob" shall be transformed and God will regenerate the entire cosmos through this people's restoration.

> Now if their transgression is riches for the world (*cosmos*) and their failure is riches for the Gentiles, how much more will their fulfillment be! For if their rejection is the reconciliation of the world (*cosmos*), what will their acceptance be but life from the dead? (Romans 11:12,15)

Like many, I am convinced that the pre-incarnate Messiah was the agent of Jacob's metamorphosis. In like manner, He will bring the age long struggle between Jacob's God and His people ("Jacob") to a conclusion. Jesus said of His Father,

> Have you not read what was spoken to you by God: "I AM ... THE GOD OF JACOB"? (Matthew 22:31b-32a)

In Genesis, it seems as if the God of Jacob waited for the patriarch to come to a place of despair. His doom was certain. Esau wanted to kill him. Jacob knew he could. In that night, Jacob not only came face to face with God, but with himself. In seeing himself in the light of the "face of God" he was broken and re-formed.

> He said, "Your name shall no longer be Jacob, but Israel; for you have striven with God and with men and have prevailed."
>
> Then Jacob asked him and said, "Please tell me your name." But he said, "Why is it that you ask my name?" And he blessed him there.

> So Jacob named the place Peniel, for he said, "I have seen God face to face, yet my life has been preserved" (Genesis 32:28-30).

Jacob's God was willing to wait for the opportune time to ambush and conquer the patriarch. He is as determined to wrestle and transform the Jewish people as He was their ancestor. He was Jacob's Deliverer. He is Jacob's Deliverer. He will be Jacob's Deliverer. He does not change. The Living God still loves "Jacob."[92]

> For thus says the LORD, "Sing aloud with gladness for Jacob, and shout among the chief of the nations; Proclaim, give praise and say, 'O LORD, save Your people, the remnant of Israel.' (Jeremiah 31:7)

We have just settled that "Israel" is synonymous with "Jacob" signifying the Jewish people. Next comes the task of identifying the "Deliverer."

What is a "Deliverer?" Who is "the Deliverer?"

16

The Redeemer, Part 3: What is a "Redeemer?"

IN HEBREW THE PRIMARY WORD FOR "REDEEMER" IS "*goel.*"[93] A *goel* is someone who, as a kinsman, buys something back. He redeems it either because he is the original owner, or because he is acting in the original owner's place. *Goel* can also mean, "deliverer." The Greek word, "*ruomai,*" translates *goel* in both the New Testament and the Septuagint. What does *ruomai/goel* mean? What does a redeemer deliver, and what does a deliverer redeem? In the remainder of these chapters I will use the words "deliverer" and "redeemer" interchangeably.

Paul anticipated the Jewish people's restoration. Although he recognized a redemptive progression, his hope was focused on a person, not a process. He stressed that Israel shall be personally delivered by their covenant keeping Redeemer.

To describe God and His interaction with humanity, the Scriptures employ culturally defined roles and relationships. When the prophets wrote of God and Israel being Husband and wife, that metaphor is best understood within the context of Israel's culture at the time the oracle was communicated. These varied earthly pictures illustrate human interaction with the sublime. Humanity, as God's image, is perfectly formed to illustrate the relationship of the Creator to Himself and creation. In the midst of the nations, God's intentionally formed people were handcrafted to make specific realities known.

> The people whom I formed for Myself will declare My praise (Isaiah 43:21).

It is within biblical culture that we find out what a Deliverer-Redeemer is.

The Role and the Relationship:

What is redeemed?

The *goel's* responsibility was recognized by his community. He was to "redeem" his family, or family's property, from bondage or trouble. As such, the *goel* was generally a relative. He had a privileged place in the redemption of property. He had an obligation to uphold the structure of his society as he looked after the welfare of his family and tribe. If a relative sold a field to ease financial pressure, at the appropriate opportunity, the redeemer was to repurchase the property. The same was true for a relative who had sold himself into slavery for financial reasons. The relative-redeemer was responsible for his family's liberation (Leviticus 25:25, 48).

The original owner of livestock had a right to buy back animals that, as a tithe, were dedicated to God. There was some sort of "tax" on this. Some think it was to avoid cheating. I believe the increased price reflected the dedicated animal's increased value because it had been given to God (Leviticus 27:11).

In the case of manslaughter, not premeditated murder, it was not the community's role to exact justice. Balancing the scales was the responsibility of the redeemer (in this case *goel* is translated "avenger" of blood). As the near relative, the same rules applied to the avenger (*goel*) of blood as in the buying back of a family's field, or an enslaved family member (Numbers 35:12).

The Emotionally Engaged Redeemer

In human terms a redeemer is always relationally involved. A case can be made that the *goel* is often emotionally engaged as well. It is true that both the avenger of blood and the levirate marriage could be "honor" motivated. However, at times the emotional aspects are rich. Of course, motivations of honor and other feelings can be active simultaneously. Perhaps the most emotionally charged role is what is called the "avenger of blood." The opposite end of the emotional spectrum can be seen in the book of Ruth. Boaz, Ruth's *goel*, fell in love with her. Boaz explained his intentions to Ruth and described a possible hurdle. He said:

> Now it is true I am a close relative (*goel*); however, there is a relative (*goel*) closer than I (Ruth 3:12).

Boaz overcame the obstacles and married the woman of his dreams. He was her deliverer-redeemer (*goel*).

Here are some examples of the emotional content of the deliverer-redeemer's actions.

The redeemer (*goel*) says,

> *"That's our family's land. We love our inheritance. I will buy it back. It's a matter of honor and love for our family. Redeeming this land establishes righteousness in the community. Wisdom dictates that this land is necessary to provide for our family's future. I have the right to buy it back. I have the means. I shall do it."*

The deliverer (*goel*) says,

> *"She is my brother's widow. There are no children to carry on his legacy and strengthen our clan. That is heartbreaking. I will marry her and make sure he has an heir."*

The redeemer (*goel*) says,

> *"That is my relative who is enslaved. I will buy him back."*

The avenger (*goel*) of blood says,

> *"That was a member of my beloved family who was killed. I shall execute justice and exact vengeance. Vengeance is mine."*

When Isaiah prophesied of Jacob's coming Deliverer, the people knew what he was talking about. Within this culture the emotional and relational involvement of the *Goel* was self-evident.

Jacob's Deliverer in Isaiah

> *In the Scriptures, God amply demonstrated and proclaimed that He is "Israel's Redeemer."*

In the Scriptures, God amply demonstrated and proclaimed that He is "Israel's Redeemer." When Isaiah prophesied to Israel, he often referred to God as their *Goel.*[94] When God calls Himself Jacob-Israel's Redeemer-deliverer, He is not just describing His activities. This word opens up a window for those who desire to see Him as He is. He is revealing His relationship and emotional ties to Jacob. God paid a price to redeem Israel. He exemplified the enculturated roles that were legislated in Torah.

There is a wealth of scriptural background to Paul's stated expectation. For example, in Isaiah's writings the prophet connected the Divine Redeemer and His redeeming actions to "Jacob" seven times. Here they are:

To begin, Jacob, a "worm," is to place total confidence in the LORD, the Holy One of Israel who is their Redeemer.

> "Do not fear, you worm Jacob, you men of Israel; I will help you," declares the LORD, "and your Redeemer is the Holy One of Israel" (Isaiah 41:14).

The LORD is the Creator of Jacob. He formed Israel. He has redeemed and called Jacob by name and Jacob belongs to God.

> But now, thus says the LORD, your Creator, O Jacob, and He who formed you, O Israel, "Do not fear, for I have redeemed you; I have called you by name; you are Mine! (Isaiah 43:1)

Both heaven and earth are called to rejoice. Why? The LORD has redeemed Jacob and shows His glory in Israel.

> Shout for joy, O heavens, for the LORD has done it! Shout joyfully, you lower parts of the earth; Break forth into a shout of joy, you mountains, O forest, and every tree in it; for the LORD has redeemed Jacob and in Israel He shows forth His glory (Isaiah 44:23).

The whole world is to know and rejoice in the LORD's redeeming His servant, Jacob.

> Go forth from Babylon! Flee from the Chaldeans! Declare with the sound of joyful shouting, proclaim this, send it out to the end of the earth; say, "The LORD has redeemed His servant Jacob" (Isaiah 48:20).

God is going to violently judge Israel's oppressors to the degree that the whole of mankind shall recognize that the LORD is their Savior and Redeemer. He is the Mighty One of Jacob.

> I will feed your oppressors with their own flesh, and they will become drunk with their own blood as with sweet wine; and all flesh will know that I,

> the LORD, am your Savior and your Redeemer, the Mighty One of Jacob (Isaiah 49:26).

The Redeemer is going to respond to the repentance of the Remnant of Jacob. He is going to come to Zion.

> "A Redeemer will come to Zion, and to those who turn from transgression in Jacob," declares the LORD (Isaiah 59:20).

When the nations turn to bless Israel, they are going to know that the LORD is Israel's Savior and Redeemer. He is the Mighty One of Jacob.

> You will also suck the milk of nations and suck the breast of kings; then you will know that I, the LORD, am your Savior and your Redeemer, the Mighty One of Jacob (Isaiah 60:16).

Let's sum that up. Is there a pattern that can be discerned?

Yes, there is. According to Isaiah, Jacob, a "worm," is to place total confidence in the LORD, the Holy One of Israel, who is their Redeemer (41:14). Why? Because the LORD is the Creator of Jacob. He formed Israel. He has redeemed and called Jacob by name and Jacob belongs to God (43:1). Ultimately, both heaven and earth are called to rejoice because the LORD has redeemed Jacob, and upon that redemption's foundation, shows His glory in Israel (44:23). In fact, the whole world is to know and rejoice in the LORD's redemption of His servant, Jacob (48:20). They shall know this because God is going to violently judge Israel's oppressors. These tyrants will be judged to the extent that the whole of mankind shall recognize that the LORD is Jacob's savior and redeemer. He is the Mighty One of Jacob (49:26).

Israel's recognition of God's saving acts will provoke their Redeemer to respond to the repentance of the remnant of

Jacob. He is going to come to Zion (59:20). When the nations turn to bless Israel, they are going to know that the LORD is Israel's Savior and Redeemer. He is the Mighty One of Jacob (60:16).

The Right of Redemption

God is still Israel's Deliverer. How do we know? Paul reinforced this reality in Romans 11. Inspired by Isaiah, he prophesied of the return of Jacob's Heavenly Redeemer.

> And so all Israel will be saved; just as it is written, "THE DELIVERER WILL COME FROM ZION, HE WILL REMOVE UNGODLINESS FROM JACOB." "THIS IS MY COVENANT WITH THEM, WHEN I TAKE AWAY THEIR SINS" (Romans 11:26-27).

Remember, one did not appoint oneself as a *goel.* There were recognized rules to this intrinsic relationship. Here are two Scriptures that speak of the "right of redemption." Boaz's relative did not want to redeem family land because he would have to marry Ruth. He said to Boaz,

> Redeem it for yourself; you may have my right of redemption (Ruth 4:6b).

Jeremiah's cousin came requesting that the prophet would exercise his familial right of redemption.

> Then Hanamel my uncle's son came ... and said to me, "Buy my field, please, that is at Anathoth...for you have the right of possession and the redemption is yours; buy it for yourself" (Jeremiah 32:8).

What right does God have to act as a kinsman to Jacob? There is a history to this. Jacob classified the Angel of the LORD as someone who redeemed, or delivered him from evil.

> The angel who has redeemed me from all evil, Bless the lads; and may my name live on in them, and the names of my fathers Abraham and Isaac; and may they grow into a multitude in the midst of the earth (Genesis 48:16).

Isaiah spoke of God's extraordinary empathy and emotional involvement that motivated His delivering acts.

> In all their affliction He was afflicted, and the angel of His presence saved them; in His love and in His mercy He redeemed them, and He lifted them and carried them all the days of old (Isaiah 63:9).

This is axiomatic: the degree of love influences the choices one makes on behalf of the beloved. What amazing faithful love God has for His people! Not only has He *not* rejected them, but He has made known the outcome of His determined love. He is not content to allow the Jewish people to slide off the stage of history. He is going to leave heaven and deliver His people. The portrayal of the Lord's last action before the outcome of "life from the dead" is dramatic. Use your imagination.

Not only has He not rejected them, but God has made known the outcome of His determined love. He is not content to allow the Jewish people to slide off the stage of history. He is going to deliver His people.

Jesus, the Deliverer, comes from heaven and rescues Jacob. He removes Jacob's sin. Then a covenantal transformation transpires. He is still Jacob's Redeemer.

In the Messiah Jesus, God is incarnate as a member of Jacob's family. He has the right to redeem. It is worth noting that the Messianic Deliverer (*Goel*) is both "Redeemer" and "Avenger of Blood." He is Israel's nearest relative who reigns in heaven. The Jewish people are family who are in bondage. He will fulfill His role as Redeemer and liberate them. Israel has been hounded by the nations. God has the responsibility to "avenge" this persecuted people.

17

The Redeemer, Part 4: The Year of Redemption

CLOSELY CONNECTED TO THE ROLE OF THE "AVENGER of blood" is the "year of redemption."

> For the day of vengeance was in My heart, and My year of redemption has come (Isaiah 63:4).

Isaiah 63:4 specifically has to do with the avenging of blood. It is a very powerful image. Imagine the emotional background for the use of this metaphor. The "year of redemption" is in parallel to the "day of vengeance." This is a particularly violent phrase. Jesus said that, in the midst of end-time trials, believers should look up because their redemption draws near. From my perspective, this is most likely referencing the same event. Here's the section in Isaiah 63 where we can see the emotional state of the Redeemer/Deliverer:

> Who is this who comes from Edom, with garments of glowing colors from Bozrah, this One who is majestic in His apparel, marching in the greatness of His strength?
>
> "I have trodden the wine trough alone, and from the peoples there was no man with Me. I also trod them in My anger and trampled them in My wrath; and their lifeblood is sprinkled on My garments, and I stained all My raiment. For the day of vengeance was in My heart, and My year of redemption has come. I looked, and there was no one to help, and I was astonished and there was

> no one to uphold; so My own arm brought salvation to Me, and My wrath upheld Me. I trod down the peoples in My anger and made them drunk in My wrath, and I poured out their lifeblood on the earth."
>
> I shall make mention of the lovingkindnesses of the LORD, the praises of the LORD, according to all that the LORD has granted us, and the great goodness toward the house of Israel, which He has granted them according to His compassion and according to the abundance of His lovingkindnesses (Isaiah 63:3-7).

Now look at the Messiah's words from Luke 21:

> There will be great distress upon the land and wrath to this people; and they will fall by the edge of the sword, and will be led captive into all the nations; and Jerusalem will be trampled underfoot by the Gentiles until the times of the Gentiles are fulfilled.
>
> There will be signs in sun and moon and stars, and on the earth dismay among nations, in perplexity at the roaring of the sea and the waves, men fainting from fear and the expectation of the things which are coming upon the world; for the powers of the heavens will be shaken.
>
> Then they will see THE SON OF MAN COMING IN A CLOUD with power and great glory. But when these things begin to take place, straighten up and lift up your heads, because your redemption is drawing near (Luke 21:23b-28).

At the end of this age the times of the Gentiles will be fulfilled. The Jewish disciples were called to take courage and look up in the midst of all manner of cosmic disruption. Jesus said that their redemption was coming. The reason their "redemption is drawing near" is because the "Redeemer will come" (Isaiah 59:20-21; Romans 11:26-27). This "redemption" is the coming "day of vengeance" when God removes iniquity from Jacob and brings them into a transgenerational experience of the New Covenant.

Jacob shall be delivered. He shall be liberated from spiritual slavery and delivered from oppressive demonic principalities and their international human proxies.

Jacob shall be delivered. He shall be liberated from spiritual slavery and delivered from oppressive demonic principalities and their international human proxies.

This:

> Again he says, "REJOICE, O GENTILES, WITH HIS PEOPLE" (Romans 15:10)...

Alludes to this:

> Rejoice, O nations, with His people; for He will avenge the blood of His servants, and will render vengeance on His adversaries, and will atone for His land and His people (Deuteronomy 32:43).

God shall atone for His land and His people. Jacob shall be delivered from "his" sins and be brought into a renewed covenant with the Deliverer.

Allusions

The New Testament contains many quotations from the Old Testament. It is often the case that these references allude to the sections of Scripture in which these quotes are found. To ignore these hints is to impoverish our understanding of the apostolic worldview and the point of the quotation. Here are a couple of illustrations of this from the Gospels.

Jesus' Crucifixion

When He was crucified, Jesus quoted Psalm 22:1. This is the verse:

> My God, my God, why have You forsaken me? Far from my deliverance are the words of my groaning (Psalm 22:1).

Here is where Jesus quoted them:

> About the ninth hour Jesus cried out with a loud voice, saying, "ELI, ELI, LAMA SABACHTHANI?" that is, "MY GOD, MY GOD, WHY HAVE YOU FORSAKEN ME?" (Matthew 27:46)

The Messiah knew that His suffering and humiliation had been described centuries earlier. When He quoted Psalm 22:1, the entire psalm was brought to the minds of those who knew the Scriptures.

When we read of this:

> And when they had crucified Him, they divided up His garments among themselves by casting lots ... (Matthew 27:35)

We are intended to remember these verses from Psalm 22:

> I am poured out like water, and all my bones are out of joint; my heart is like wax; it is melted within me. My strength is dried up like a potsherd, and my tongue cleaves to my jaws; and You lay me in the dust of death.
>
> For dogs have surrounded me; a band of evildoers has encompassed me; they pierced my hands and my feet. I can count all my bones. They look, they stare at me; they divide my garments among them, and for my clothing they cast lots (Psalm 22:14-18).

When this happened:

> In the same way the chief priests also, along with the scribes and elders, were mocking Him and saying, "He saved others; He cannot save Himself. He is the King of Israel; let Him now come down from the cross, and we will believe in Him. HE TRUSTS IN GOD; LET GOD RESCUE Him now, IF HE DELIGHTS IN HIM; for He said, 'I am the Son of God'" ... (Matthew 27:41-43)

For those with "eyes to see," these words would be remembered:

> All who see me sneer at me; they separate with the lip, they wag the head, saying, "Commit yourself to the LORD; let Him deliver him; let Him rescue him, because He delights in him" (Psalm 22:7-8).

Psalm 22 prerecorded the Messiah's despair, humiliation, and His glorious resurrection vindication. For those who were well taught in the Scriptures, it didn't take more than a couple of citations to direct the hearers' attention to the entire passage.

Jesus' Suffering and Glory

Here is another example. John alluded to all of Isaiah 53 and Isaiah 6 when he wrote of the Messiah's rejection:

> This was to fulfill the word of Isaiah the prophet which he spoke: "LORD, WHO HAS BELIEVED OUR REPORT? AND TO WHOM HAS THE ARM OF THE LORD BEEN REVEALED?"
>
> For this reason they could not believe, for Isaiah said again, "HE HAS BLINDED THEIR EYES AND HE HARDENED THEIR HEART, SO THAT THEY WOULD NOT SEE WITH THEIR EYES AND PERCEIVE WITH THEIR HEART, AND BE CONVERTED AND I HEAL THEM."

> These things Isaiah said because he saw His glory, and he spoke of Him (John 12:38-41).

John connected the glory of the pre-incarnate Messiah revealed to Isaiah with the Messianic humility manifest at the Crucifixion. He expected his readers to know Isaiah 6 and 53 and, understanding the fullness of their contexts, see Jesus' pre-incarnate glory connected to His suffering.

Here's another example of the writers of the New Testament displaying familiarity with Isaiah 53. Matthew 8:17 quoted Isaiah 53:4.

> When evening came, they brought to Him many who were demon-possessed; and He cast out the spirits with a word, and healed all who were ill. This was to fulfill what was spoken through Isaiah the prophet: "HE HIMSELF TOOK OUR INFIRMITIES AND CARRIED AWAY OUR DISEASES" (Matthew 8:16-17).

Matthew was pointing his readers to all of Isaiah 53. He placed Jesus' healing ministry in the framework of His atoning work. It is recognized that the author of Matthew was probably a Jewish disciple writing within a community of Messianic Jews. The author expected his readers to be familiar with this prophecy.

The Context of the Oracle is Important

When we read Paul's quotation of the Hebrew Scriptures, we should look at the quotation's context. The ubiquitous Augustinian quote, "The Old is the New concealed. The New is the Old revealed" has a lot of truth in it. However, who decided the content of what the "New" revealed? Interpreters of the New Testament are generally hostile towards the plain meaning of the very Scriptures upon which the Apostolic Writings rely. Their original contexts speak of God's relationship with Israel. Rarely looking to the framework in which these oracles are found, they plant them within the commonly held presupposition of supersessionism.

What is the foundational setting of Romans 11:26-27? Here are those verses again:

> And so all Israel will be saved; just as it is written, "THE DELIVERER WILL COME FROM ZION, HE WILL REMOVE UNGODLINESS FROM JACOB." "THIS IS MY COVENANT WITH THEM, WHEN I TAKE AWAY THEIR SINS" (Romans 11:26-27).

When Paul wrote this, he was primarily leaning upon Isaiah 59:20. Here is the immediate context of that oracle:

> So they will fear the name of the LORD from the west and His glory from the rising of the sun, for He will come like a rushing stream which the wind of the LORD drives.
>
> "A Redeemer will come to Zion, and to those who turn from transgression in Jacob," declares the LORD.
>
> "As for Me, this is My covenant with them," says the LORD: "My Spirit which is upon you, and My words which I have put in your mouth shall not depart from your mouth, nor from the mouth of your offspring, nor from the mouth of your offspring's offspring," says the LORD, "from now and forever" (Isaiah 59:19-21).

Remember, Paul wrote, "...this is My covenant with them, when I take away their sins" (Romans 11:27). According to Paul's source, Isaiah, the covenant Paul prophesied is a renewed promise of an everlasting transgenerational relationship of Israel with God. Furthermore, this section serves as an introduction into a description of what that outworking of this transgenerational covenant shall be like. That description is found in the immediately following verses (Isaiah 60). Let's study this section of Romans by surveying Isaiah 59:16-60:22.

The immediate precursor to the Scripture Paul quotes has to do with God the Warrior coming to Israel's rescue. He promises to come with great fury, and the deliverance He brings shall bring great glory from the nations.

> And He saw that there was no man, and was astonished that there was no one to intercede; then His own arm brought salvation to Him, and His righteousness upheld Him.
>
> He put on righteousness like a breastplate, and a helmet of salvation on His head; and He put on garments of vengeance for clothing and wrapped Himself with zeal as a mantle.
>
> According to their deeds, so He will repay, wrath to His adversaries, recompense to His enemies; to the coastlands He will make recompense. So they will fear the name of the LORD from the west and His glory from the rising of the sun, for He will come like a rushing stream which the wind of the LORD drives.

This shall happen because the Redeemer will come.

> "A Redeemer will come to Zion, and to those who turn from transgression in Jacob," declares the LORD.

The Deliverer's work is connected with the establishing of a new covenant with the Jewish people.

> "As for Me, this is My covenant with them," says the LORD: "My Spirit which is upon you, and My words which I have put in your mouth shall not depart from your mouth, nor from the mouth of your offspring, nor from the mouth of your

> offspring's offspring," says the LORD, "from now and forever."

The result of the redemption and the renewed relationship is described immediately afterwards. In Isaiah 60 we receive more insight into the Messianic hope of Israel. Is it presumptuous to believe that Paul knew Isaiah 60? No, it is not. Paul knew the verses that followed Isaiah 59 and pointed to them when he wrote Romans 11:26-27. Look at Paul's expectation.

First, Paul believed that the glory of the LORD would arise upon a Redeemed Jacob dwelling in the midst of a darkened cosmos.

> Arise, shine; for your light has come, and the glory of the LORD has risen upon you. For behold, darkness will cover the earth and deep darkness the peoples; but the LORD will rise upon you and His glory will appear upon you (Isaiah 60:1-2).

He believed that the Gentiles would come to "Jacob's" light and that through their ministry the exile of the Jewish people would come to an end. There is a geographic aspect to Paul's expectation.

> Nations will come to your light, and kings to the brightness of your rising (v. 3).
>
> Lift up your eyes round about and see; they all gather together, they come to you. Your sons will come from afar, and your daughters will be carried in the arms. Then you will see and be radiant, and your heart will thrill and rejoice; because the abundance of the sea will be turned to you, the wealth of the nations will come to you (vs. 4-5).

Here is another reference to the land of Israel, specifically, Jerusalem, in Paul's expectation. God's worship shall be enhanced at the place of His throne, Jerusalem.

> And I shall glorify My glorious house (v.7).

18

The Redeemer, Part 5: The Glorious Conclusion

A COMPLETE TRANSFORMATION OF INTERNATIONAL relationships shall happen when the King's glory is seen on the people of Israel.

> Who are these who fly like a cloud and like the doves to their lattices?
>
> Surely the coastlands will wait for Me; and the ships of Tarshish will come first, to bring your sons from afar, their silver and their gold with them, for the name of the LORD your God, and for the Holy One of Israel because He has glorified you.
>
> Foreigners will build up your walls, and their kings will minister to you; for in My wrath I struck you, and in My favor I have had compassion on you.

God's wrath is turned away, for the Redeemer has come and removed ungodliness from Jacob. The result is that Israel shall no longer be despised and oppressed. Instead, there shall be a continual stream of pilgrims to the place of manifest glory.

> Your gates will be open continually; they will not be closed day or night, so that men may bring to you the wealth of the nations, with their kings led in procession. For the nation and the kingdom

> which will not serve you will perish, and the nations will be utterly ruined.

There shall be restitution and reconciliation of the nations who "afflicted" the Jewish people.

> The glory of Lebanon will come to you, the juniper, the box tree and the cypress together, to beautify the place of My sanctuary; and I shall make the place of My feet glorious. The sons of those who afflicted you will come bowing to you, and all those who despised you will bow themselves at the soles of your feet; and they will call you the city of the LORD, the Zion of the Holy One of Israel.

Paul said that the Deliver would remove Jacob's iniquity and establish a renewed covenant with the Jewish people. According to Isaiah, what happens next? This: the peace of the age-to-come will be fully manifest. The following verses are a blueprint for the reiterated oracles given to us in Revelation's description of the New Jerusalem (Revelation 22:5).

> Whereas you have been forsaken and hated with no one passing through, I will make you an everlasting pride, a joy from generation to generation...then you will know that I, the LORD, am your Savior and your Redeemer, the Mighty One of Jacob...and I will make peace your administrators and righteousness your overseers. Violence will not be heard again in your land, nor devastation or destruction within your borders; but you will call your walls salvation, and your gates praise. No longer will you have the sun for light by day, nor for brightness will the moon give you light; but you will have the LORD for an everlasting light, and your God for your glory. "Your sun will no longer set, nor will your moon wane; for you will have the LORD for an

> everlasting light, and the days of your mourning will be over (Isaiah 60:15, 16b, 17b-20).

God is really going to bless Israel. It shall be "life from the dead."

Then all your people will be righteous; they will possess the land forever, the branch of My planting, the work of My hands, that I may be glorified. The smallest one will become a clan, and the least one a mighty nation. I, the LORD, will hasten it in its time (Isaiah 60:21-22).

When Paul affirmed Isaiah's foretelling of the coming Deliverer (Isaiah 59:20), he pointed to the description of the glory of the coming age found in Isaiah 60. It is a prophecy of the glorious fulfillment of God's promises. It is the foretelling of the restoration of all things of which the prophets spoke (Acts 3:21). It is what Paul understood when he quoted the previous verses found at the end of Isaiah 59. It is the aftermath of what "all Israel" being saved shall look like.

Paul believed in God's utter faithfulness to Israel. According to the apostle, all of the Jewish people are beloved for the sake of the Patriarchs and the promises, gifts, and election are irrevocable. That is the nature of God's love for the Jewish people. He is a transgenerational God who is devoted to Israel. Like Job, Israel can say, "I know that my Redeemer lives." This confidence shall ultimately be rewarded. The prosperity of Israel shall overflow to the rest of the world. As God's election of this people is honored during the age-to-come, the nations shall be blessed. The nations shall

> *All of the Jewish people are beloved for the sake of the Patriarchs and the promises, gifts, and election are irrevocable. That is the nature of God's love for the Jewish people.*

partake of the blessing that they bestow. What they sow, they shall reap, pressed down, shaken together and running over. It is called "greater riches" for a reason.

The transnational Church is partnering with God for the hastening of this day. The "fullness of the Gentiles" shall come in through the fulfillment of the Great Commission. The church's intercession for, and ministry to, the Jewish people shall bear fruit. There shall be greater riches. There shall be life from the dead.

Who is the Deliverer? Where is He From?

I'm certain that those who have read this book are positive that the Deliverer is the Messiah, Jesus. 1 Thessalonians 1:10 explicitly confirms that. The synergy of these two verses are mutually beneficial. Romans 11:26-27 gives more context to the apostolic view of the Second Coming described in 1 Thessalonians 1:10. Here are the two complementary Scriptures speaking of the Deliverer and His work:

> And so all Israel will be saved; just as it is written, "THE DELIVERER WILL COME FROM ZION, HE WILL REMOVE UNGODLINESS FROM JACOB. THIS IS MY COVENANT WITH THEM, WHEN I TAKE AWAY THEIR SINS" (Romans 11:26-27).

> And to wait for his Son from heaven, whom he raised from the dead, Jesus our deliverer from the coming wrath (1 Thessalonians 1:10, NET).

The primary verse Paul cited in Romans 11:27 is from Isaiah 59. However, we do not want to overlook the fact that he also works with Psalms 14:7 and 53:6. Those verses are identical.

Here they are:

> Oh, that the salvation of Israel would come out of Zion! When God restores His captive people, Jacob will rejoice, Israel will be glad (Psalm 14:7; 53:6).

Working with Psalm 14:7, Psalm 53:6, and the Septuagint's translation of Isaiah 59:20, Paul provided a composite quotation that reminded the Romans that the Deliverer will come from Zion and remove ungodliness from Jacob. Here are the citations from the Psalms, Isaiah 59:20-21 (from the Hebrew), Isaiah 59:20 (from the Septuagint) and the Romans passage.

Here are the verses Paul wisely used from the Hebrew version of Isaiah 59:20-21:

> A Redeemer will come to Zion, and to those who turn from transgression in Jacob," declares the LORD. "As for Me, this is My covenant with them," says the LORD: "My Spirit which is upon you, and My words which I have put in your mouth shall not depart from your mouth, nor from the mouth of your offspring, nor from the mouth of your offspring's offspring," says the LORD, "from now and forever" (Isaiah 59:20-21).

This is from the Septuagint's version of Isaiah 59:20:

> And the deliverer shall come for Sion's sake, and shall turn away ungodliness from Jacob (Isaiah 59:20 LXE).

The verses from the Psalms:

> Oh, that the salvation of Israel would come out of Zion! When God restores His captive people, Jacob will rejoice, Israel will be glad (Psalm 14:7; 53:6).

Here is Paul's composite quotation:

> And so all Israel will be saved; just as it is written, "THE DELIVERER WILL COME FROM ZION, HE WILL REMOVE UNGODLINESS FROM JACOB."
>
> "THIS IS MY COVENANT WITH THEM, WHEN I TAKE AWAY THEIR SINS" (Romans 11:26-27).

Please note that the Deliverer is identified in 1 Thessalonians 1:10. The New English Translation gracefully renders the Greek:

> And to wait for his Son from heaven, whom he raised from the dead, Jesus our deliverer from the coming wrath (1 Thessalonians 1:10 NET).

Through 1 Thessalonians 1:10 the location of the "Zion" from which the Redeemer will come is reinforced. Jesus, the Deliverer, comes from heaven. Remember, at the time Paul wrote 1 Thessalonians the transnational Church was overwhelmingly ethnically Jewish. These Messianic Jews awaited their Deliverer. What did they expect the Deliverer to do? They expected Jesus to come and sanctify their nation, delivering them from the oppressive wicked cultures of the surrounding nations. Paul utilized Psalm 14 to describe the iniquity-infused hostile cultures in which Israel's godly remnant and holy Gentile converts found themselves. In Romans 3:10-12 Paul applied Psalm 14 as part of a chain of references denouncing both pagan culture and hostile majority-Israel. When Paul quoted part of Psalm 14, he alluded to the whole psalm. He returns to Psalm 14 in Romans 11:26. Here is Psalm 14:

> The fool has said in his heart, "There is no God." They are corrupt, they have committed abominable deeds; there is no one who does good.
>
> The LORD has looked down from heaven upon the sons of men to see if there are any who understand, who seek after God. They have all

> turned aside, together they have become corrupt; there is no one who does good, not even one.
>
> Do all the workers of wickedness not know, who eat up my people as they eat bread, and do not call upon the Lord? There they are in great dread, for God is with the righteous generation.
>
> You would put to shame the counsel of the afflicted, but the LORD is his refuge.
>
> Oh, that the salvation of Israel would come out of Zion! When the LORD restores His captive people, Jacob will rejoice, Israel will be glad (Psalm 14:1-7).

Pay attention to the conclusion of this foundational psalm. Salvation will come out of Zion; the Deliverer comes from Zion. At the end of the age, the LORD will restore His captive people. As a result, "Jacob will rejoice, Israel will be glad."

> And so all Israel will be saved; just as it is written, "THE DELIVERER WILL COME FROM ZION, HE WILL REMOVE UNGODLINESS FROM JACOB."
>
> "THIS IS MY COVENANT WITH THEM, WHEN I TAKE AWAY THEIR SIN (Romans 11:26-27).

> *A primary aspect of the Second Coming is Israel-oriented. The Deliverer comes in glory to rescue believers from the wrath to come as He delivers Israel.*

A primary aspect of the Second Coming is Israel-oriented. The Deliverer of whom Paul wrote in 1 Thess. 1:10 and Romans 11:26-27 is the same person. He comes in glory to rescue believers from the wrath to come as He delivers Israel. The Deliverer/Redeemer (*Goel*) is Jesus. Romans 11:26-27 refers to the Messiah's return (1 Thessalonians 1:10a).

Intercede that this day would happen soon. The psalmist yearned for it. Paul did, too. So should we. Let Paul's longing affirm and fuel our intercession.

> Oh, that the salvation of Israel would come out of Zion! When God restores His captive people, Jacob will rejoice, Israel will be glad (Psalm 14:7; 53:6).

O come, and let us marvel together:

> Oh, the depth of the riches both of the wisdom and knowledge of God! How unsearchable are His judgments and unfathomable His ways! For WHO HAS KNOWN THE MIND OF THE LORD, OR WHO BECAME HIS COUNSELOR? Or WHO HAS FIRST GIVEN TO HIM THAT IT MIGHT BE PAID BACK TO HIM AGAIN? For from Him and through Him and to Him are all things. To Him *be* the glory forever. Amen (Romans 11:33-36).

19

What Now?

MY HOPE IS THAT THIS BOOK ENCOURAGED YOU AND provided you with nourishment for your head and heart. It would be wonderful if what is written here fortifies and equips you for more effective prayer. I also hope the information in these chapters strengthens your understanding and helps you "teach others also" (2 Timothy 2:2).

God's purposes for the Jewish people will come to pass. How? I don't know the details. This story comes to mind:

> Then Elisha said, "Listen to the word of the LORD; thus says the LORD, 'Tomorrow about this time a measure of fine flour will be *sold* for a shekel, and two measures of barley for a shekel, in the gate of Samaria.'"
>
> The royal officer on whose hand the king was leaning answered the man of God and said, "Behold, if the LORD should make windows in heaven, could this thing be?"
>
> Then he said, "Behold, you will see it with your own eyes, but you will not eat of it." (2 Kings 7:1-2)

In response to the promises God has made, I feel a bit like the "royal officer" in this story. However, the prophet was vindicated and the naysayer was trampled in the rush of a famished people's desperation to obtain provision. I am assured that God's heart will be satisfied. He is motivated by love and His purposes will be fulfilled. A glorious destiny awaits the Jewish people and all those who are "fellow-citizens with the saints" (Eph. 2:19).

God is motivated by love and His purposes will be fulfilled. A glorious destiny awaits the Jewish people and all those who are "fellow-citizens with the saints."

I do not claim that everything I've written is absolutely true. I sincerely believe that I "know in part" (1 Corinthians 13:9, 12) and part of that "knowing" is not knowing when what I believe is wrong. However, in good conscience, I think that in these pages a faithful testimony to the apostles' outlook has been maintained and shared with you.

The prophets' and apostles' words are not obsolete. This remains certain:

> Glorious things are spoken of you, O city of God. Selah (Psalm 87:3).

Since these things are so, then, despite my inability to foresee how they shall come to pass, I maintain that the "windows of heaven" shall be opened. God is going to pour out a holy revival that is going to sweep the people of Israel into a full participation in the Kingdom of God. It shall be "life from the dead" (Romans 11:15b).

God is going to pour out a holy revival that is going to sweep the people of Israel into a full participation in the Kingdom of God. It shall be "life from the dead."

> What then shall we say to these things? (Romans 8:31a)

Here's what I say:

I believe the Church is not going to succumb to insecurity and hubris. Instead, I believe the Church is going to grow in the personal and corporate knowledge of the Messiah's love. I expect that this transformation will prepare them for fellowship with the God of Abraham, Isaac, and Jacob's heart concerning His people, Israel. A people secure in the Messiah's love will be able to identify with that which God loves, and it is written that God loves the Jewish people "for the sake of the Patriarchs" (Romans 11:28).

Here is a prophetic strategy I would like to encourage:

> For thus says the LORD, "Sing aloud with gladness for Jacob, and shout among the chief of the nations; Proclaim, give praise and say, 'O LORD, save Your people, the remnant of Israel'" (Jeremiah 31:7).

God's promises are sure. Therefore, before we see the full answer to our prayers, let us demonstrate the age-to-come and join together with confident expectation.

> REJOICE, O GENTILES, WITH HIS PEOPLE (Romans 15:10b).

The remnant of Israel receives your fellowship in our common hope.

> Now if their transgression is riches for the world and their failure is riches for the Gentiles, how much more will their fulfillment be!
>
> But I am speaking to you who are Gentiles. Inasmuch then as I am an apostle of Gentiles, I magnify my ministry, if somehow I might move to jealousy my fellow countrymen and save some of them. For if their rejection is the reconciliation of the world, what will *their* acceptance be but life from the dead? (Romans 11:12-15)

> *I encourage you to share the word of life to all those around you, prioritizing the Jewish people according to Romans 1:16.*

Right now, God is preparing the foundation for this massive movement of the Jewish people to the Messiah. At this time I encourage you to share the word of life to all those around you, prioritizing the Jewish people according to Romans 1:16:

> For I am not ashamed of the gospel, for it is the power of God for salvation to everyone who believes, to the Jew first and also to the Greek (Romans 1:16).

Let's end with this doxology:

> Now to Him who is able to keep you from stumbling, and to make you stand in the presence of His glory blameless with great joy, to the only God our Savior, through Jesus [the] Messiah our Lord, *be* glory, majesty, dominion and authority, before all time and now and forever. Amen (Jude 1:24-25).

About the Author

David and his wife, Elaine, have led Restoration Fellowship in Glen Cove, New York, since the mid 1970's. He is the author of the book, *God's True Love* and leads the *Love of God Project* which serves the believing community through instruction and releasing impartation concerning God's love. In addition, he offers a weekly podcast: *Love and War with David Harwood.* A Jewish believer, David is ordained through The Lamb's Chapel (Moravian Falls, NC) and received a Masters of Professional Studies from the Alliance Theological Seminary in Nyack, NY.

Since 2006 the Love of God Seminar has been given one-on-one, and to churches, Messianic synagogues, leadership teams, ministry networks, and ministry training schools. There is a video small group curriculum available through their website: loveofgodproject.org

The Love of God Project is based in Restoration Fellowship, and is affiliated with Tikkun, a Messianic Jewish network.

David and Elaine are parents of three wonderful grown children: Shira, Jonathan (with his exceptional wife, Gina) and Benjamin.

Acknowledgments

I wanted the book to be vetted by an evangelical minister, a historic church priest and a Messianic rabbi. So, I asked Pastor David Herling, Father Michael Paciello, and Rabbi Carl Kinbar to review the earliest attempts at expressing what I saw. Dr. Kinbar's critique of my exegesis encouraged me. David and Michael helped me prioritize the chapters. Paul Blake offered valuable initial observations and Dr. Glenn Blank, a Messianic Rabbi, helped me with editorial suggestions. Also, Pastor Charles Simpson resurrected this work after I buried it. He found it worthwhile, so I did, too. Several people helped with editing, for which I'm grateful.

Dr. Dan Juster offered encouragement. Dr. Michael Brown encouraged and fellowshipped with me along the way. A dear friend and notable servant of the Lord who recently passed away, Randall Baker, helped me put together some of these teachings as he invited me to equip intercessors concerning the relationship of Gentile and Messianic Jewish believers. Charles Simpson is responsible for getting this book edited, formatted and available. Michael Carter designed the cover. Ann Jennerjahn's edits were very helpful. I want to mention that I have friends who were emotionally wounded by some of the things I wrote. They helped sensitize me. Restoration Fellowship stood by me all the way with prayer and encouragement.

I don't know where I'd be without my wife, Elaine.

I would be remiss, and a liar, if I did not confess that, from my perspective, God helped me. My hope is that I expressed His heart by opening up the worldview of the apostles of the Messiah, Yeshua. Thank you for reading this book. *DH*

END NOTES

[1] For a quick survey of the history of the Church with the Jewish people, read Michael Brown, *Our Hands are Stained with Blood.*

[2] A discussion of the identity and characteristics of Pharisees are not in the purview of this book.

[3] Romans 11:18, 20b-21: Do not be arrogant toward the branches; but if you are arrogant, *remember that* it is not you who supports the root, but the root *supports* you…Do not be conceited, but fear; for if God did not spare the natural branches, He will not spare you, either.

[4] Romans 11:13-14: But I am speaking to you who are Gentiles. Inasmuch then as I am an apostle of Gentiles, I magnify my ministry, if somehow I might move to jealousy my fellow countrymen and save some of them.

[5] See also: Deuteronomy 4:2: You shall not add to the word which I am commanding you, nor take away from it, that you may keep the commandments of the LORD your God which I command you.

[6] 1 Timothy 4:16: Pay close attention to yourself and to your teaching; persevere in these things, for as you do this you will ensure salvation both for yourself and for those who hear you.

[7] Friberg, Timothy, and Barbara Friberg. *Analytical Greek New Testament (GNT).*

[8] For instance, Deuteronomy 28:37: You shall become a horror, a proverb, and a taunt among all the people where the LORD drives you.

[9] For the Gentiles incorporation, read: Ephesians 2:11-22; 3:3-10. To read of the representative remnant of Israel, Romans 2:28; 9:6, 27-29; 11:1-5.

[10] Brown, F., Driver, S. R., & Briggs, C. A. *Enhanced Brown-Driver-Briggs Hebrew and English Lexicon* (electronic ed.) Oak Harbor, WA. Logos Research Systems.

[11] Jeremiah employs the same word to describe the Jewish people's restoration here: 29:14; 30:3, 18; 31:23; 32:44; 33:7, 11, 26

[12] Jeremiah 49:6, 39; Ezekiel 16:53; 29:14

[13] Ps 67:4; 96:10; 110:6; Isa 2:4; Joel 3:12; Mic 4:3; Matthew 25:31-33

[14] Romans 14:10

[15] Consider Isaiah 61 in the light of Ephesians 3:20.

[16] Zechariah 12-14; Isaiah 14:24-27; Joel 3:11-21; Luke 21:24-27; Revelation 19:11-21

[17] Note the special coat and supervisory role (Genesis 37:3, 13) and the firstborn's double portion (Genesis 48:11-20).

[18] Little, Franklin. *The Crucifixion of the Jews,* Harper and Row, 1975, p. 48. Goering was a Nazi who was designated as Hitler's successor.

[19] *That Jesus Christ Was Born a Jew, Luther's Works*, American Edition (Philadelphia: Fortress Press, 1962), Volume 45, p. 201.

[20] Little, Franklin. *The Crucifixion of the Jews*, Harper and Row, 1975, p. 105.

---

[21] Luther also hated Roman Catholics, Zwinglians, Anabaptists. For a more positive assessment of Martin Luther, see Eric Metaxas' biography entitled, *Martin Luther: The Man Who Rediscovered God and Changed the World.*

22 Pietism is the name of a Lutheran spiritual renewal movement, which sought to

[22] Pietism is the name of a Lutheran spiritual renewal movement, which sought to not just know correct doctrine, but also experience the corresponding spiritual reality. One denomination that has pietistic roots is the Moravians.

[23] *The Idea of Biblical Interpretation: Essays in Honor of James L. Kugel*, Edited by Judith H. Newman, Hindy Najman, 2004, Koninklijke Brill NV, Leiden, The Netherlands, A Nazi New Testament Professor Reads His Bible: the Strange Case of Gerhard Kittel, Wayne A. Meeks, p. 515.

[24] *Roots of Theological Anti-Semitism, German Biblical Interpretation and the Jews* from Herder and Semler to Kittel and Bultmann, Anders Gerdmar, Brill, Leiden, Boston, 2009, p 423, 424.

[25] Ibid, p. 432.

[26] Kugel, Ibid, p. 516.

[27] Kugel, Ibid p. 543, 544.

[28] Kugel, Ibid, p. 540.

[29] Isaiah 24; Joel 3; Zechariah 12:1-4, 14:1-4; Revelation 19:19-21, etc.

[30] Leviticus 19:14; 21:18

[31] 1 Corinthians 13:9

[32] Hawthorne, G. F., Martin, R. P., & Reid, D. G. (1993). *Dictionary of Paul and his letters* (848). Downers Grove, IL: InterVarsity Press.

[33] Carson, D. A. (1994). *New Bible Commentary: 21st century edition* (4th ed.) (Ro 9:1–6a). Leicester, England; Downers Grove, Ill., USA: Inter-Varsity Press.

[34] Ironically, in the case of the historic churches their architecture and worship services mimic the Temple.

[35] Smyrna, Philadelphia.

[36] Ephesus: But I have this against you: You have departed from your first love! (Revelation 2:4)

[37] Louw, J. P., & Nida, E. A. (1996). *Greek-English Lexicon of the New Testament: Based on semantic domains* (electronic ed. of the 2nd edition.). New York: United Bible Societies.

[38] I will bless those who bless you, and him who dishonors you I will curse, and in you all the families of the earth shall be blessed (Genesis 12:3).

[39] For many deceivers have gone out into the world, those who do not acknowledge Jesus Christ *as* coming in the flesh. This is the deceiver and the antichrist (2 John 1:7).

[40] Craig S. Keener. *The IVP Bible Background Commentary: New Testament* (Downers Grove, Ill.: InterVarsity Press, 1993). Notes on Acts 28:31.

[41] No offense intended to any "mere" academics.

[42] Romans 11:26

[43] Exodus 20:5; James 4:5

[44] Deuteronomy 5:4-7; Exodus 19:18; 20:3

---

[45] Romans 11:8: Just as it is written, "GOD GAVE THEM A SPIRIT OF STUPOR, EYES TO SEE NOT AND EARS TO HEAR NOT, DOWN TO THIS VERY DAY.
[46] Malachi 4:5; Matthew 17:3-4
[47] "I have great sorrow and unceasing grief in my heart" (Romans 9:2). This emotion is felt keenly in the hearts of many Jewish believers and specifically called non-Jewish Christians. In fact, this book is written to you.
[48] But if some of the branches were broken off, and you, being a wild olive, were grafted in among them… (Romans 11:17a) In this verse, the word "branches" is understood. Therefore, the use of italics.
[49] This is spoken about at length in Ephesians 2 where Paul uses different metaphors.
[50] Soanes, C., & Stevenson, A. (2004). *Concise Oxford English dictionary* (11th ed.). Oxford: Oxford University Press.
[51] Merriam-Webster, I. (2003). *Merriam-Webster's collegiate dictionary.* (Eleventh ed.). Springfield, MA: Merriam-Webster, Inc.
[52] Soanes, C., & Stevenson, A. (2004). *Concise Oxford English dictionary* (11th ed.). Oxford: Oxford University Press.
[53] The Greek word is "ametameleta", the negation of "metamelomai".
[54] Thus the KJV, NAS, ESV and NKJ. Other versions follow the Hebrew more closely translating *chashaq* as "set His heart on you" (TNK, NRS, CJB, NJB) which may still be mistaken for an act of volition, not a longing desire based upon attraction that provokes the lover to initiate a binding relationship.
[55] Young's Literal Translation interprets *chashaq* as '*delighted in you.*' That is a far cry from *'set His love on you'*, and a lot closer to the verse's intent.
[56] This helpful illustration was contributed by Peter Lundgren, a messianic rabbi from NY.
[57] G. Bratcher and Howard Hatton, *A Handbook on Deuteronomy*, UBS handbook series (New York: United Bible Societies, 2000). 154.
[58] Cabal, T., Brand, C. O., Clendenen, E. R., Copan, P., Moreland, J., & Powell, D. (2007). *The Apologetics Study Bible: Real Questions, Straight Answers, Stronger Faith* (1195). Nashville, TN: Holman Bible Publishers.
[59] Brown, F., Driver, S. R., & Briggs, C. A. (2000). *Enhanced Brown-Driver-Briggs Hebrew and English Lexicon* (electronic ed.) (165). Oak Harbor, WA: Logos Research Systems.
[60] God said to Abram, "Know for certain that your descendants will be strangers in a land that is not theirs, where they will be enslaved and oppressed four hundred years. But I will also judge the nation whom they will serve, and afterward they will come out with many possessions. As for you, you shall go to your fathers in peace; you will be buried at a good old age. Then in the fourth generation they will return here, for the iniquity of the Amorite is not yet complete" (Genesis 15:13-16).
[61] Brown, F., Driver, S. R., & Briggs, C. A. (2000). *Enhanced Brown-Driver-Briggs Hebrew and English Lexicon* (electronic ed.) (990–991). Oak Harbor, WA: Logos Research Systems.

[62] Swanson, J. (1997). *Dictionary of Biblical Languages with Semantic Domains: Hebrew (Old Testament)* (electronic ed.). Oak Harbor: Logos Research Systems, Inc.
[63] Gesenius, W., & Tregelles, S. P. (2003). *Gesenius' Hebrew and Chaldee lexicon to the Old Testament Scriptures* (803). Bellingham, WA: Logos Research Systems, Inc.
[64] Smith, J. E. (1992). *The Major Prophets* (Eze 6:8–10). Joplin, Mo.: College Press.
[65] Biblical Studies Press. (2006; 2006). *The NET Bible First Edition Notes* (Eze 6:9). Biblical Studies Press.
[66] Later in this same psalm a wonderful restoration is promised: When the humble see it they will be glad; you who seek God, let your hearts revive. For the LORD hears the needy and does not despise his own people who are prisoners. Let heaven and earth praise him, the seas and everything that moves in them. For God will save Zion and build up the cities of Judah, and people shall dwell there and possess it; the offspring of his servants shall inherit it, and those who love his name shall dwell in it (Psalm 69:32-36).
[67] Romans 1:3
[68] The Greek for, "their own," is "idia." The following are some definitions from three lexicons.
[69] 2 Peter 2:6-9
[70] Revelation 20:6
[71] Matthew 25:40
[72] Keener, Craig S. *The IVP Bible Background Commentary: New Testament* (Downers Grove, Ill.: InterVarsity Press, 1993). Notes on Mt. 25:40).
[73] Barbieri, L. A., & Jr. (1985). Matthew. In J. F. Walvoord & R. B. Zuck (Eds.), *The Bible Knowledge Commentary: An Exposition of the Scriptures* (J. F. Walvoord & R. B. Zuck, Ed.) (Mt 25:31–40). Wheaton, IL: Victor Books.
[74] Blomberg, Craig. (1992). *Vol. 22*: *Matthew*. The New American Commentary (378). Nashville: Broadman & Holman Publishers.
[75] If anyone is willing to do His will, he will know of the teaching, whether it is of God or whether I speak from Myself. (John 7:17)
[76] *panta ta ethne*
[77] *panta ta ethne*
[78] *panta ta ethne*
[79] *panta ta ethne*
[80] For the list of references, go to the end of this chapter.
[81] Romans 1:16; 10:1
[82] *panta ta ethne*
[83] Not only Joel 3, but Zechariah 12-14, Isaiah 14:24-27
[84] *panta ta ethne*
[85] At the time of this writing he is in his eighties.
[86] Hans Kung, *The Church,* (New York, Sheed & Ward, 1967), p. 137.
[87] Only the Lord chose your fathers to love them, and he chose out their seed after them, *even* you, beyond all nations, as at this day (Deuteronomy 10:15, LXE)

---

[88] Galatians 3:16
[89] *panta ta ethne*
[90] Some have hopefully applied "all Israel" to every Jewish person who has ever lived. I wish! This contradicts Paul's grief and intercession found in Romans 9:1-3; 10:1.
[91] Isaiah 14:24-27; Joel 3:9-21; Zechariah 14:2-4; Luke 21:22-24; Acts 1:9-12
[92] Malachi 1:2 "I have loved you," says the LORD. But you say, "How have You loved us?" "*Was* not Esau Jacob's brother?" declares the LORD. "Yet I have loved Jacob." Matthew 22:32 "I AM...THE GOD OF JACOB"? "He is not the God of the dead but of the living."
[93] Pronounced, "Go-EL"
[94] "Your Redeemer": Isa 41:14; 43:14; 44:24; 48:17; 49:26; 54:5, 8; 60:16

Visit us at...

The Love of God Project

Educating the Body of Messiah about the love of God

http://loveofgodproject.org/

Made in the USA
Lexington, KY
02 March 2018